# INTRODUCTION

Step into a realm of timeless beauty with Volume 3 of our extraordinary collection –

"Roses in Grayscale : A Tattoo Artist's Dream in grayscale."

Immerse yourself in a breathtaking gallery of 80 photorealistic grayscale images in graphite pencil and charcoal fashion, meticulously crafted to captivate your senses and inspire your creativity.

This is a complementary version to the other two as it serve more to the artist who seeks the perfection of the roses in a book like this, and in lower budget. Make no mistake we have the same photorealistic quality in this version .

Roses in this version are a bit more open than in the other 2 versions so since roses are never enough you can still get this version too, assuming you had the other and refresh your gallery of roses with something same but different as well

Each page unveils a world of enchanting rose compositions, carefully curated to provide tattoo artists with an unparalleled resource for their craft.

From elegant single roses to intricate arrangements, these designs are tailor-made for black and grey tattoo techniques, allowing artists to masterfully play with shadow contrast and create stunning monochromatic masterpieces.

Whether you're a seasoned tattoo artist seeking fresh inspiration or an individual planning to ink a grayscale rose tattoo, either in client or for practice, this volume is a treasure trove of ready-to-tattoo designs, saving you invaluable time and unlocking a universe of artistic possibilities.

But wait there is more. This book is also made having in mind anyone that likes to express creativity with coloring books. Using your coloured pencils or markers you can create one of a kind realistic colourful roses compositions
Inside the book you will find a lesson on how to prevent colour bleeding form pages is included with full description and link to video lesson on how to easily apply it and see the results

With the purchase of this book there is also a free PDF included with many of the images from this book. It can serve as a    guide for details and or when making the stencil with PC or tablet. See instructions inside the physical book.

 Elevate your artistry and captivate your clients with this volume the ultimate resource for tattoo professionals and enthusiasts alike.

# COPYRIGHT

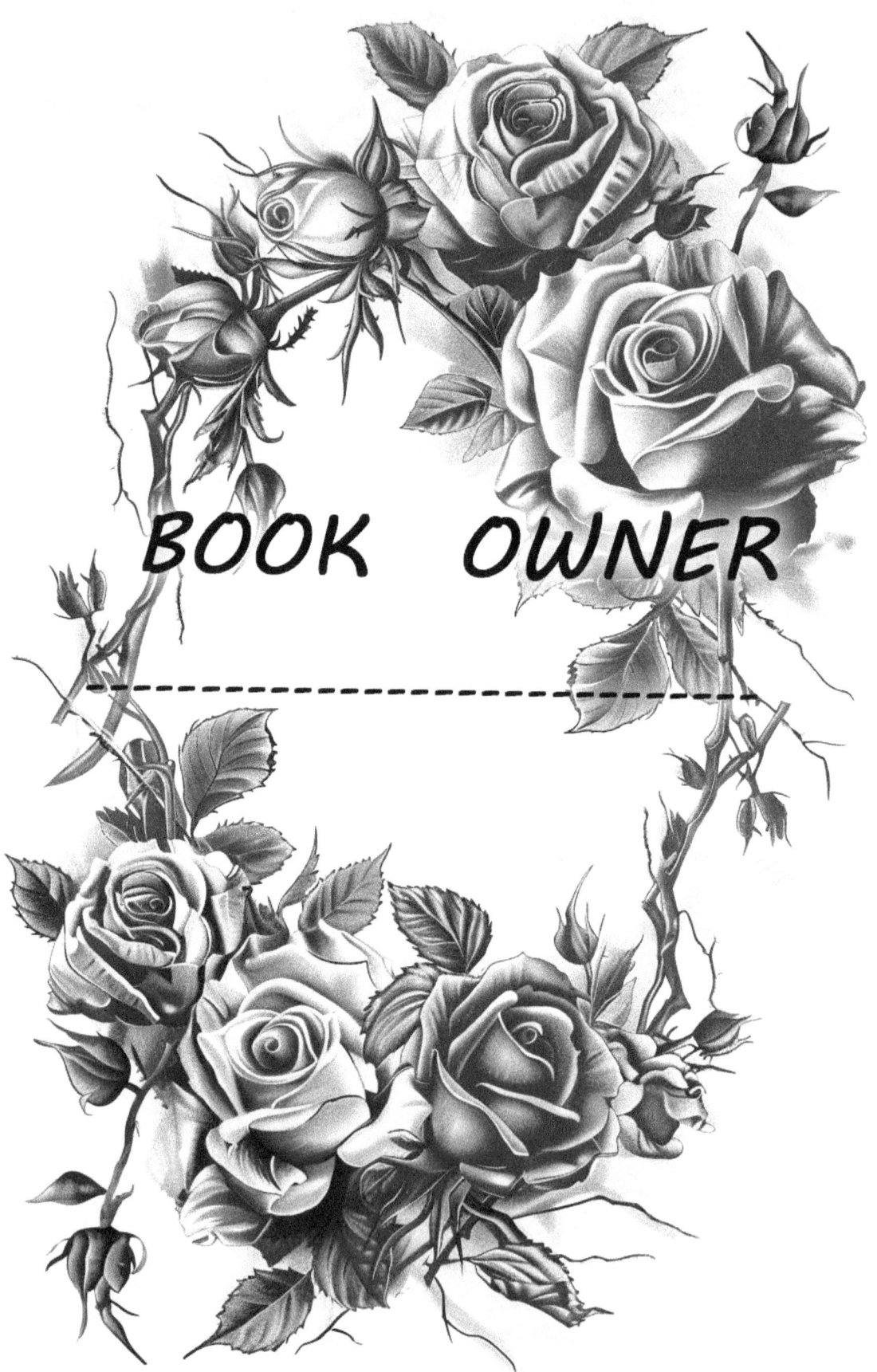

BOOK OWNER

------------

# ABOUT THE AUTHOR

Immerse yourself in the captivating world of art, where imagination knows no bounds. With over three decades of experience as a painter, tattoo artist, and author, I have dedicated my life to the pursuit of artistic excellence. Through countless hours of dedication, I have honed my skills in charcoal, pencils, and acrylic colors, specializing in the realms of realism, photorealism, and impressionism. My unique style blends elements of fantasy and impressionism, resulting in mesmerizing works of art that evoke deep emotions and leave a lasting impact.

In the realm of tattoo artistry, I have emerged as a trailblazer, revolutionizing the industry with my fresh and distinctive designs. Recognizing the need for innovation, I have created a new age of tattoo art that seamlessly combines my preferred style with eye-catching aesthetics. My designs not only captivate the eye but also empower individuals to express their individuality and uniqueness.

Expanding my creative horizons, I have delved into the world of coloring books. Gone are the days of simplistic designs with thick lines. I am on a mission to introduce the realms of realism and impressionism to the coloring book landscape. Each page of my coloring books offers intricate details and a chance for individuals to unleash their inner artist, resulting in remarkable and vibrant creations.

But my artistic endeavors don't stop there. I am currently engrossed in the creation of photo reference books that showcase wildlife and nature in unprecedented ways. These books will transport you to a world of vivid colors, breathtaking imagery, and seemingly impossible poses.

 Prepare to be captivated by the untamed beauty of the natural world, brought to life through my keen eye for detail and my passion for pushing artistic boundaries.

Join me on an awe-inspiring journey where creativity knows no limits. Together, let's explore new dimensions of artistry, where fresh perspectives, remarkable designs, and boundless inspiration await.

Welcome to my world of art, where dreams become reality, and the extraordinary is transformed into tangible beauty

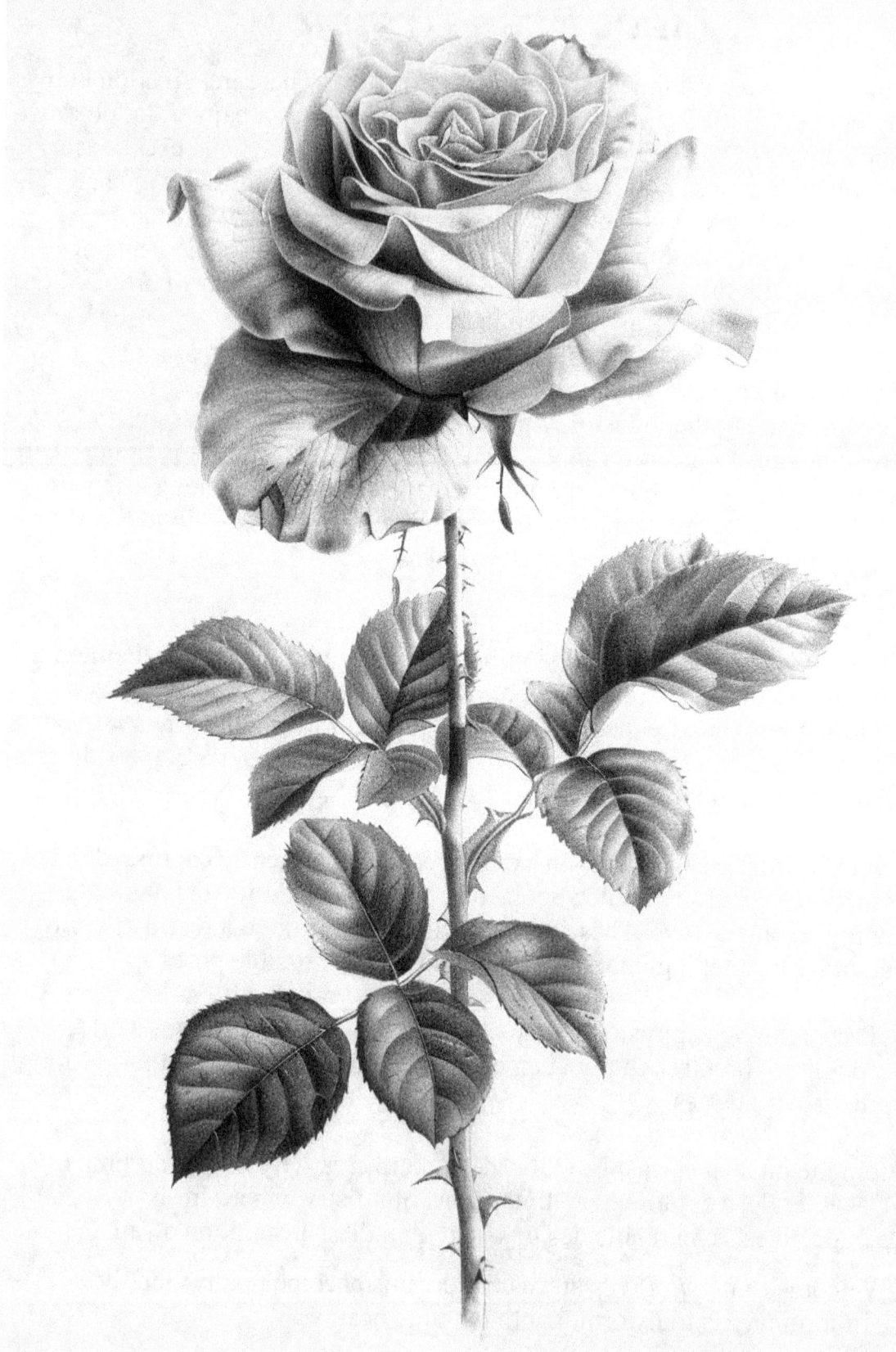

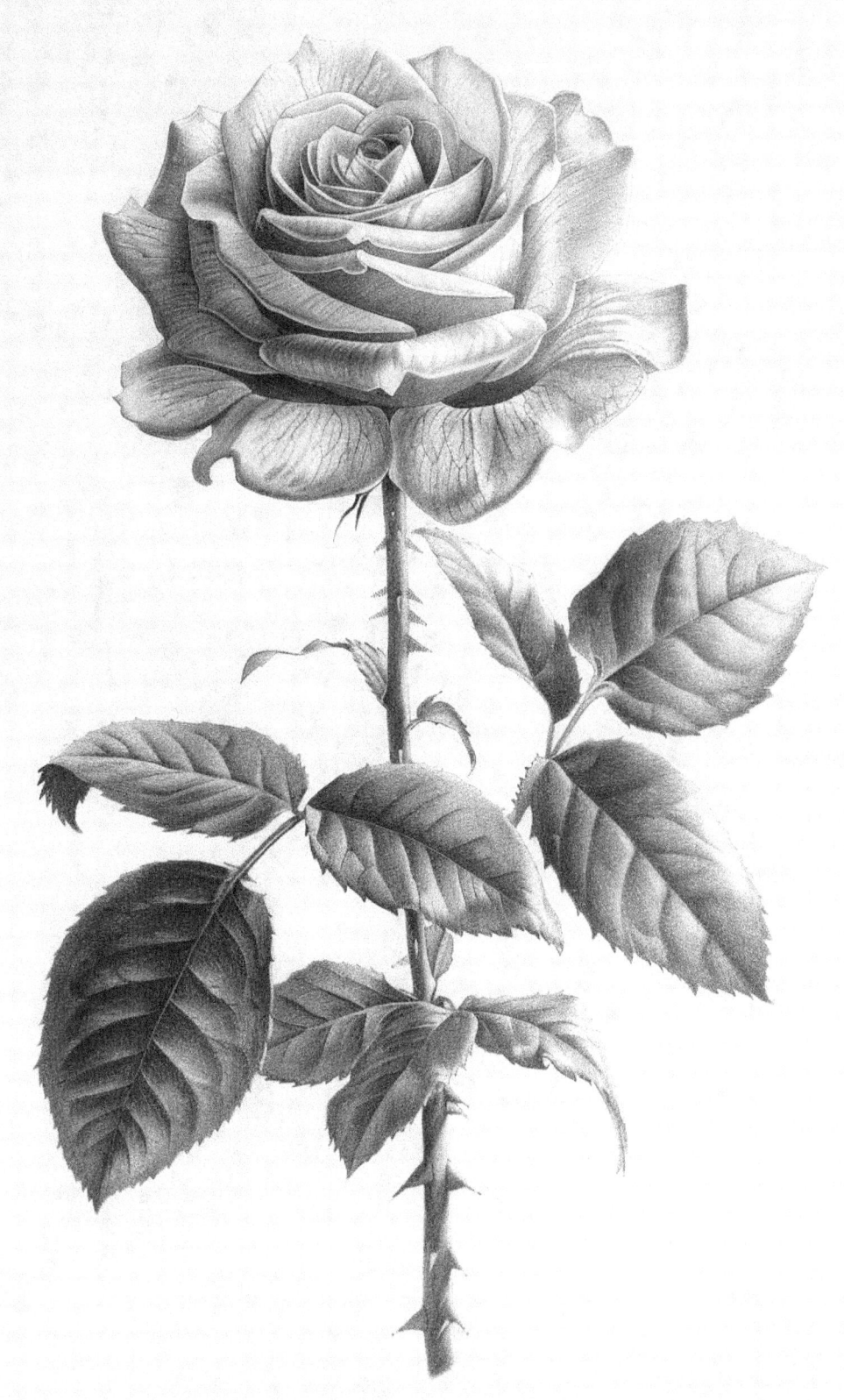

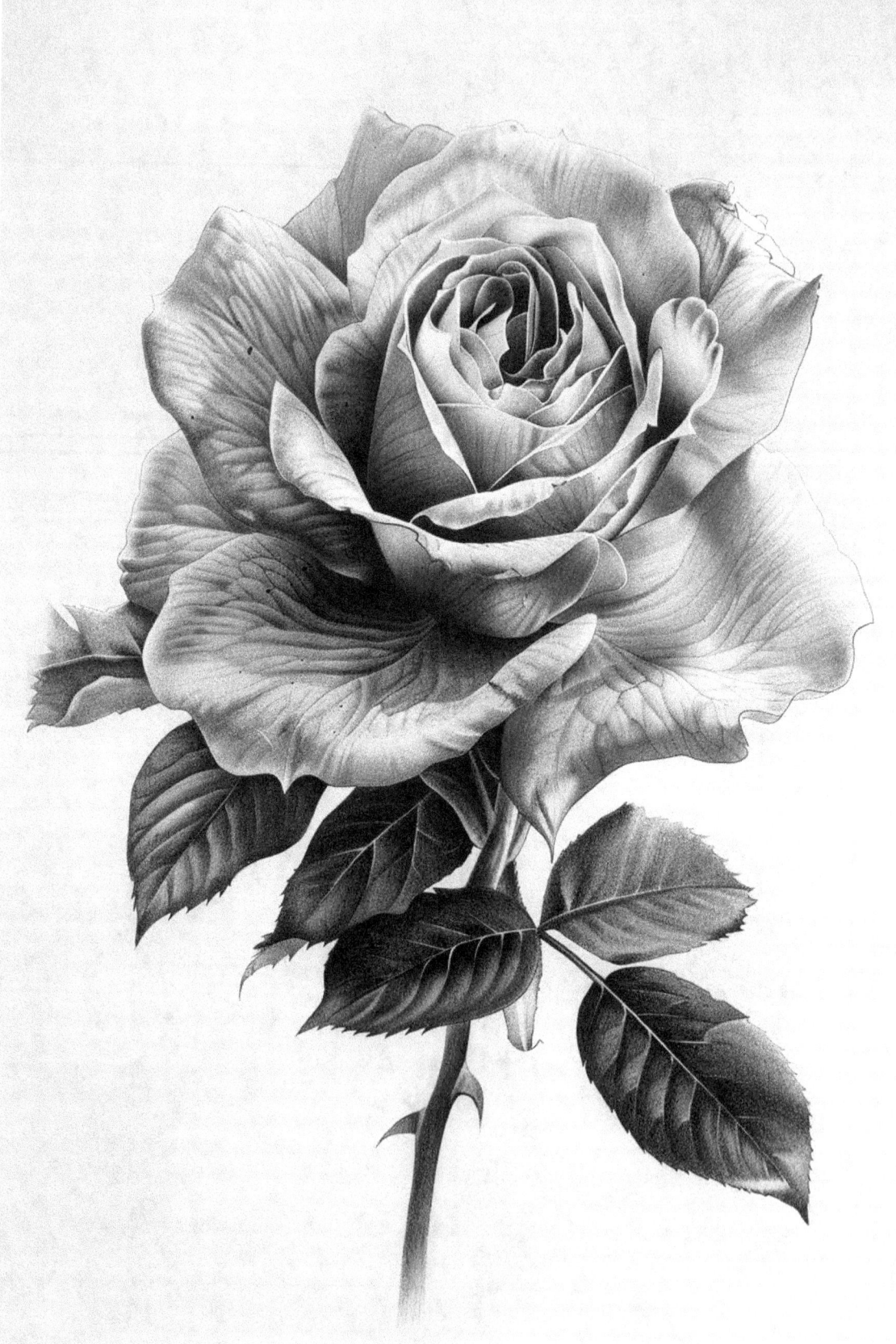

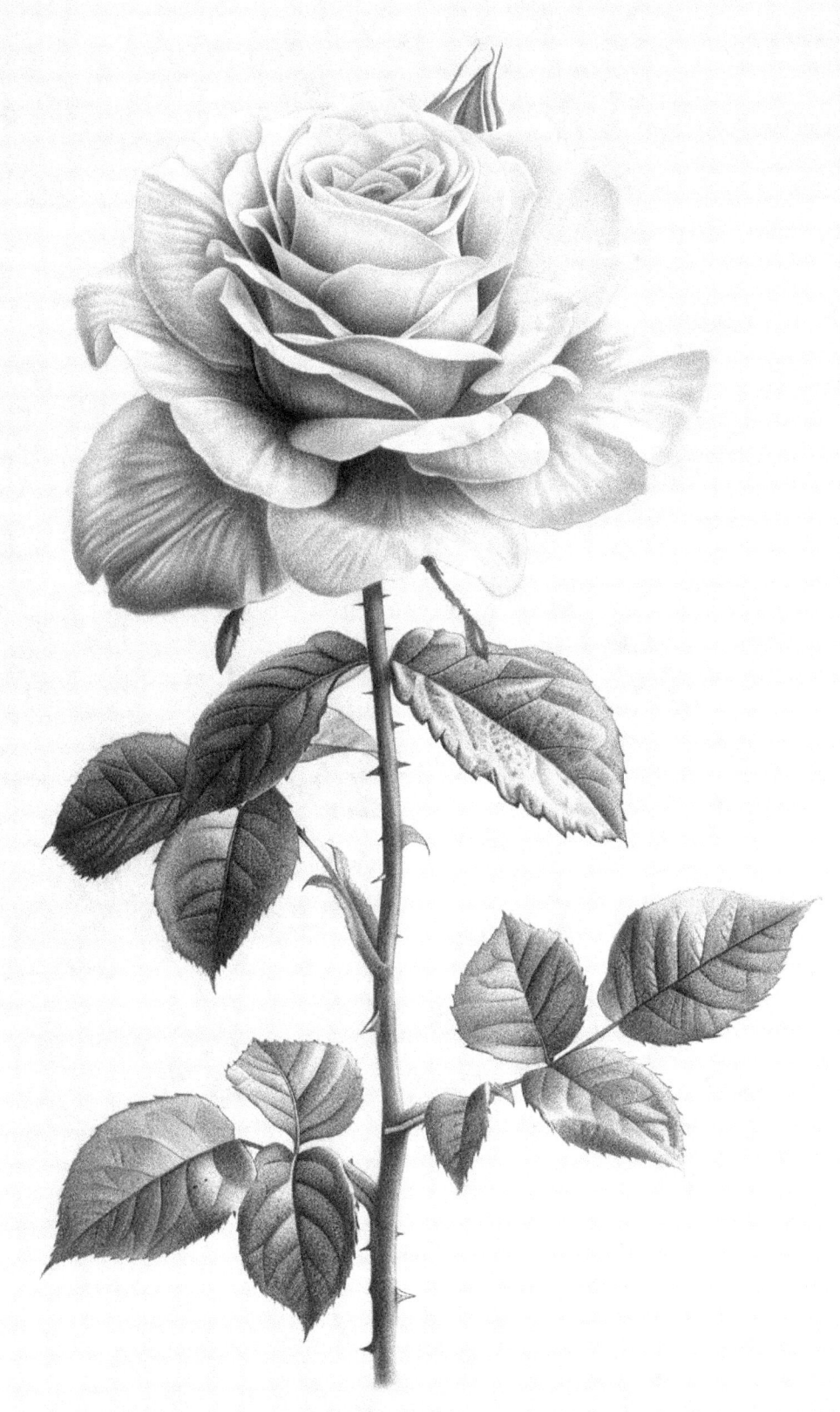

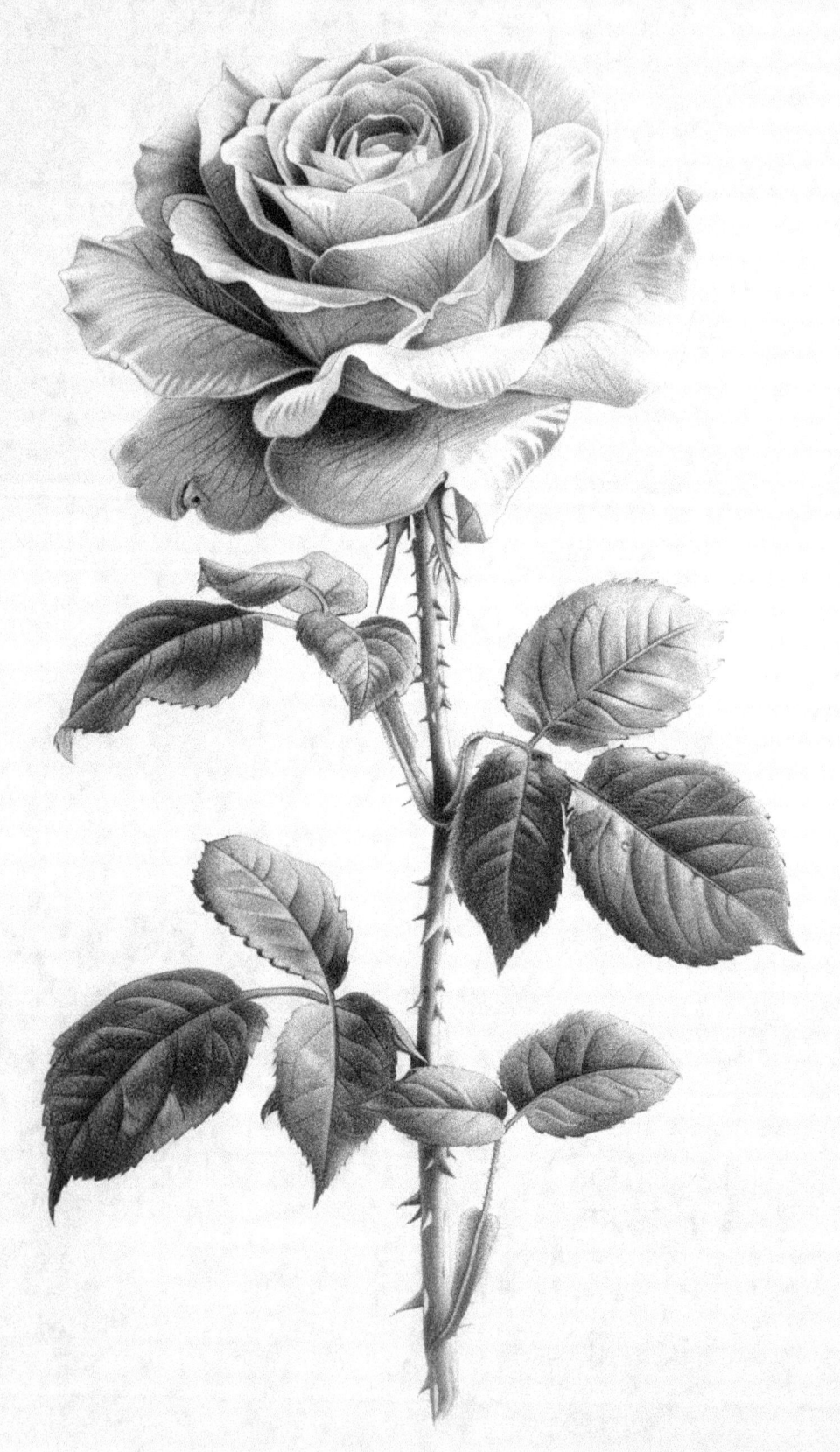

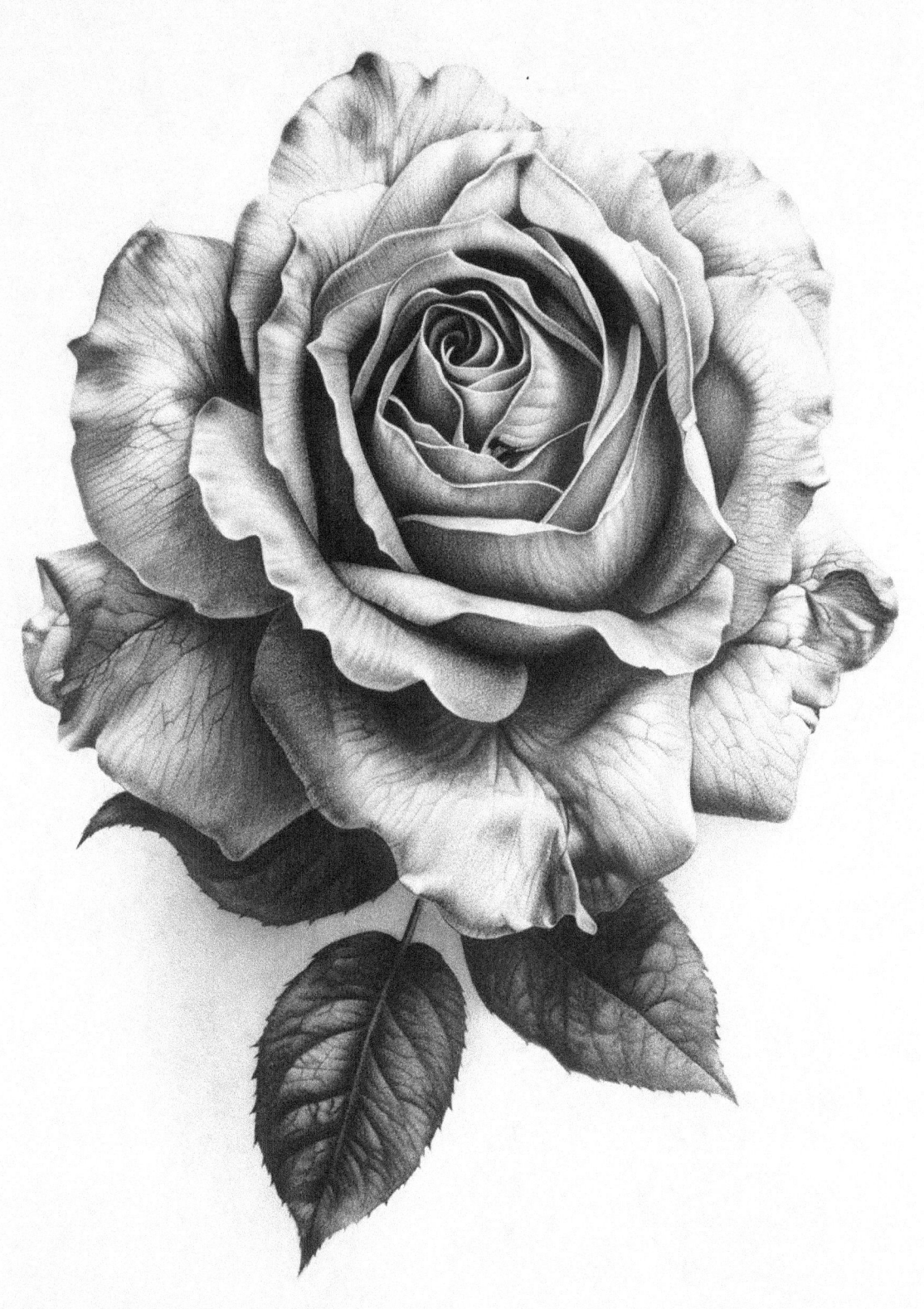

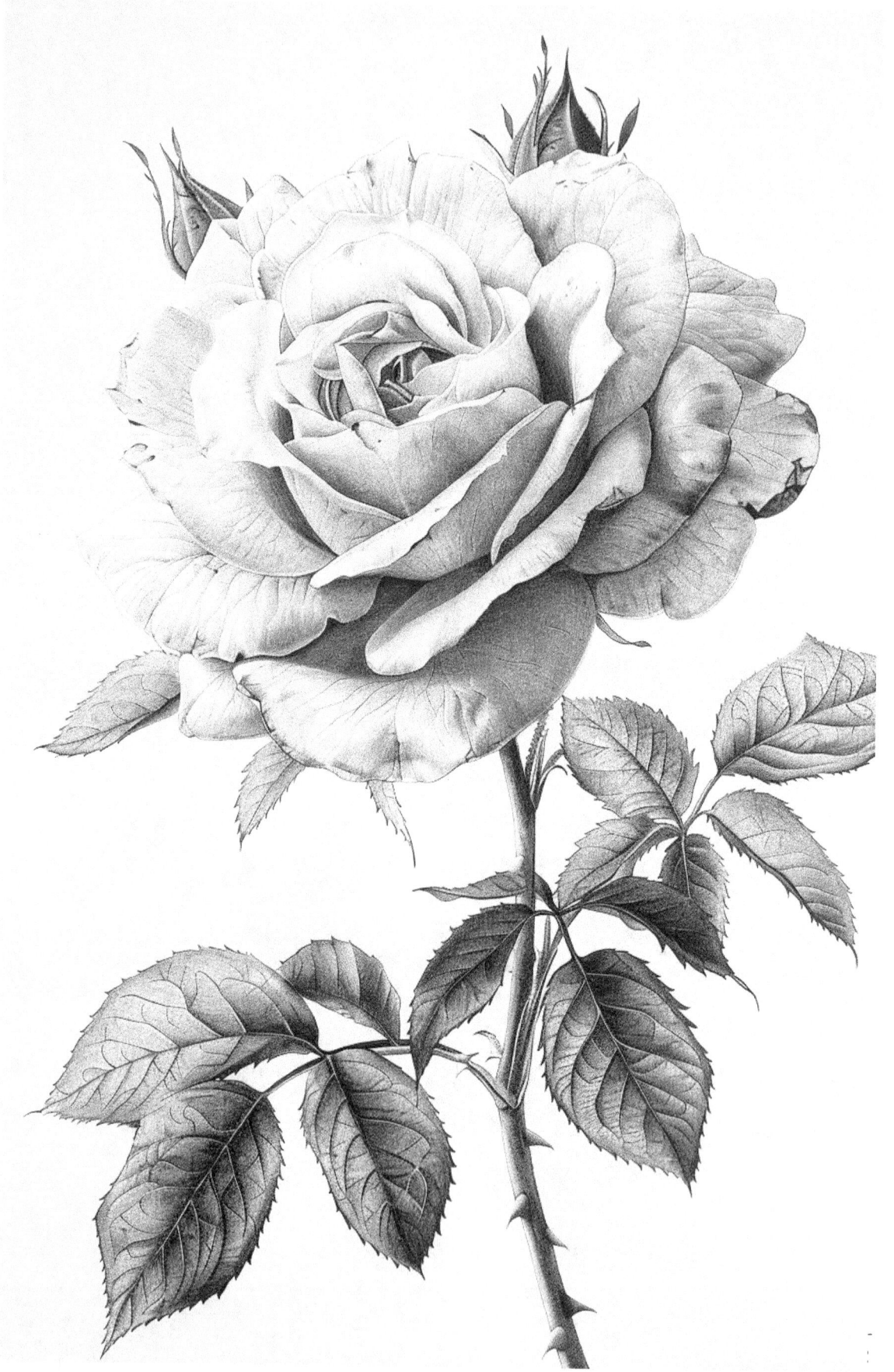

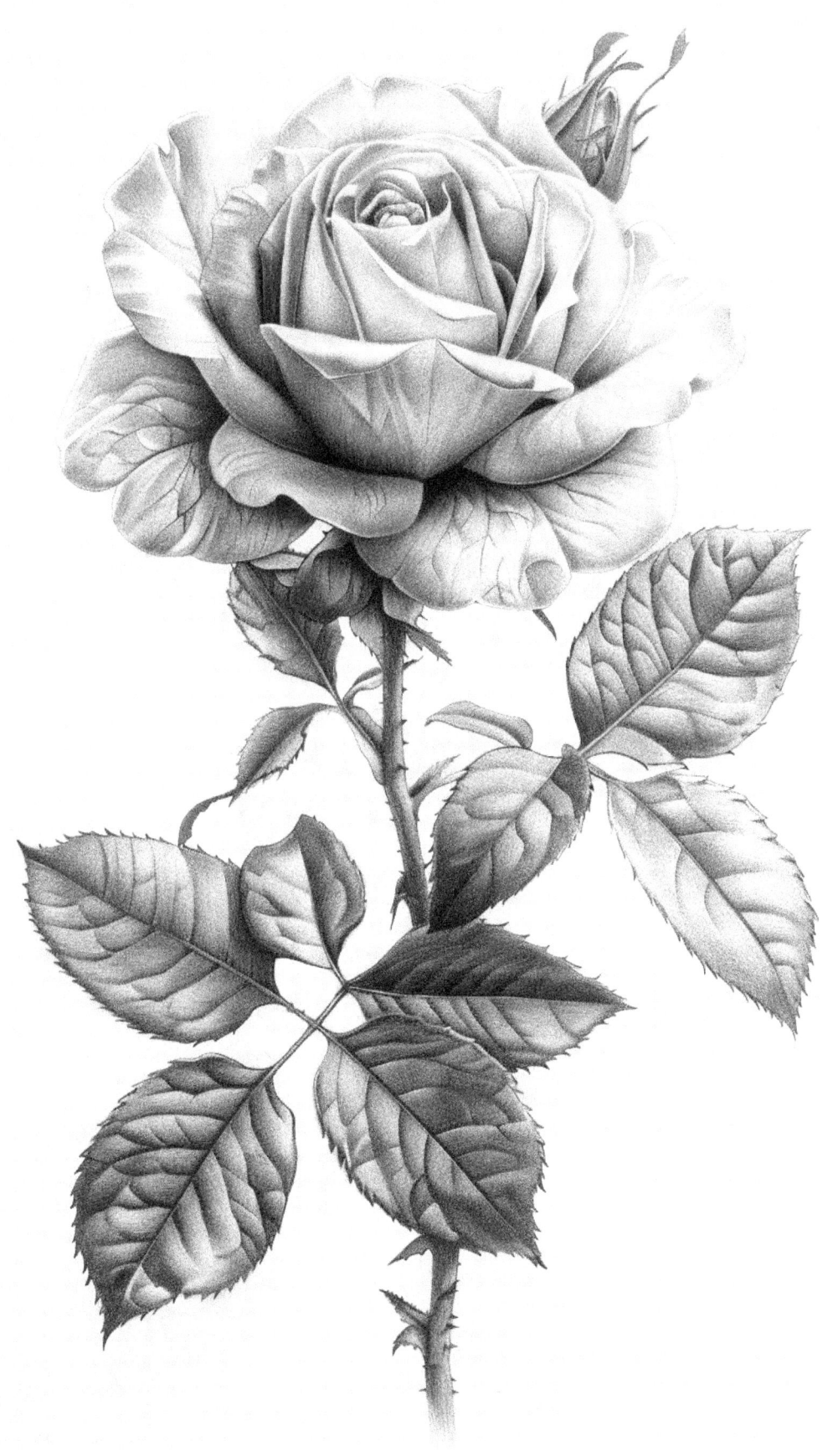

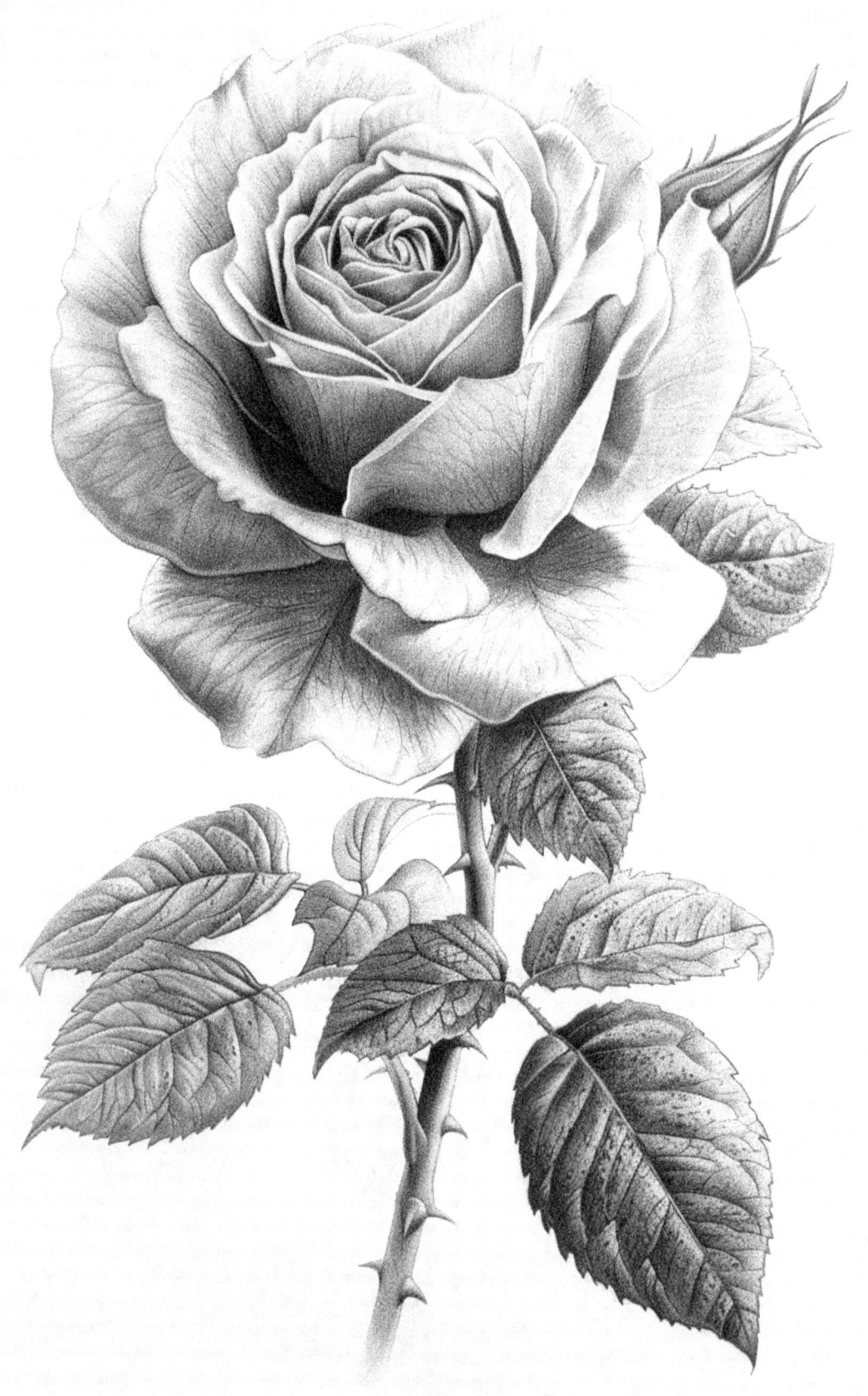

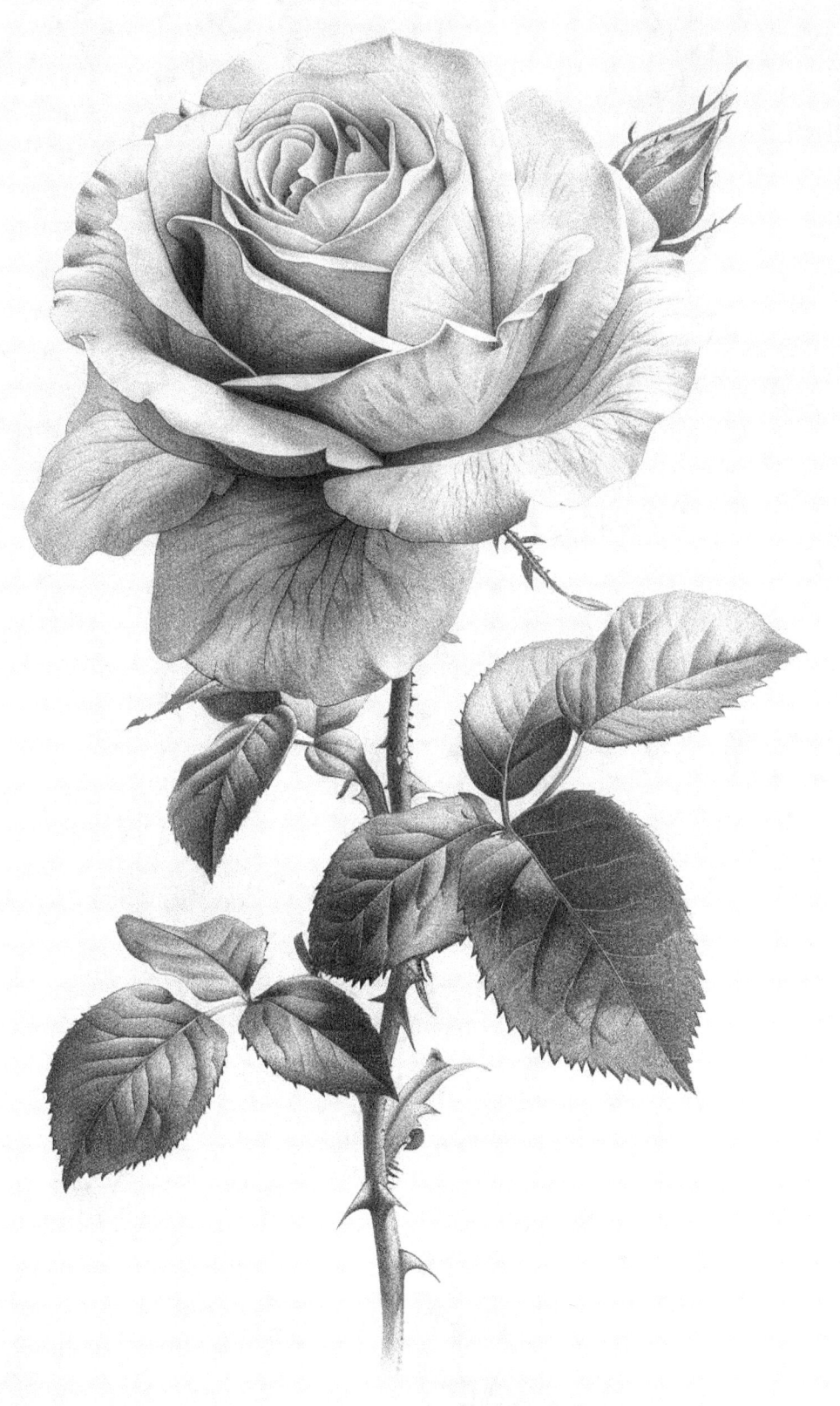

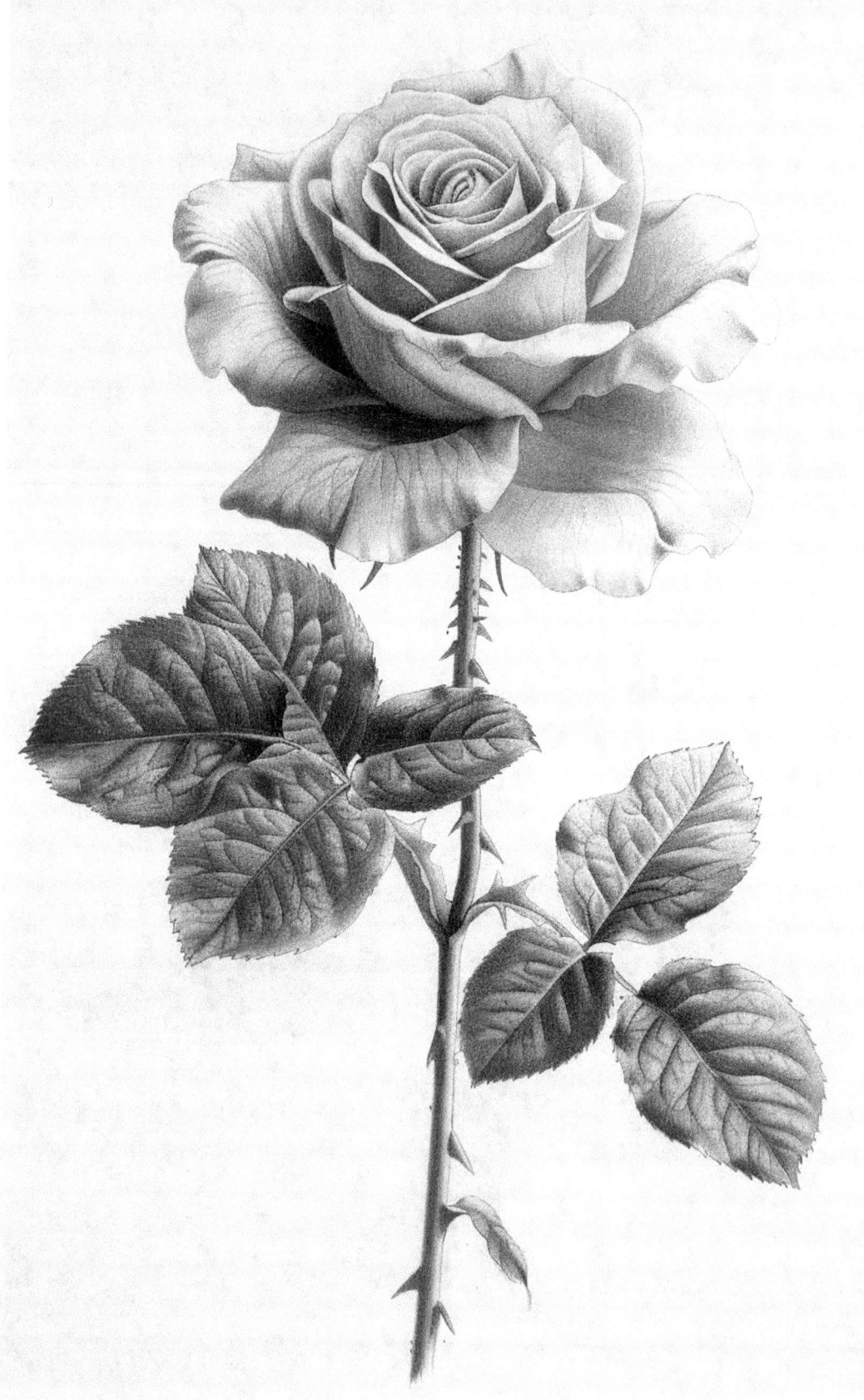

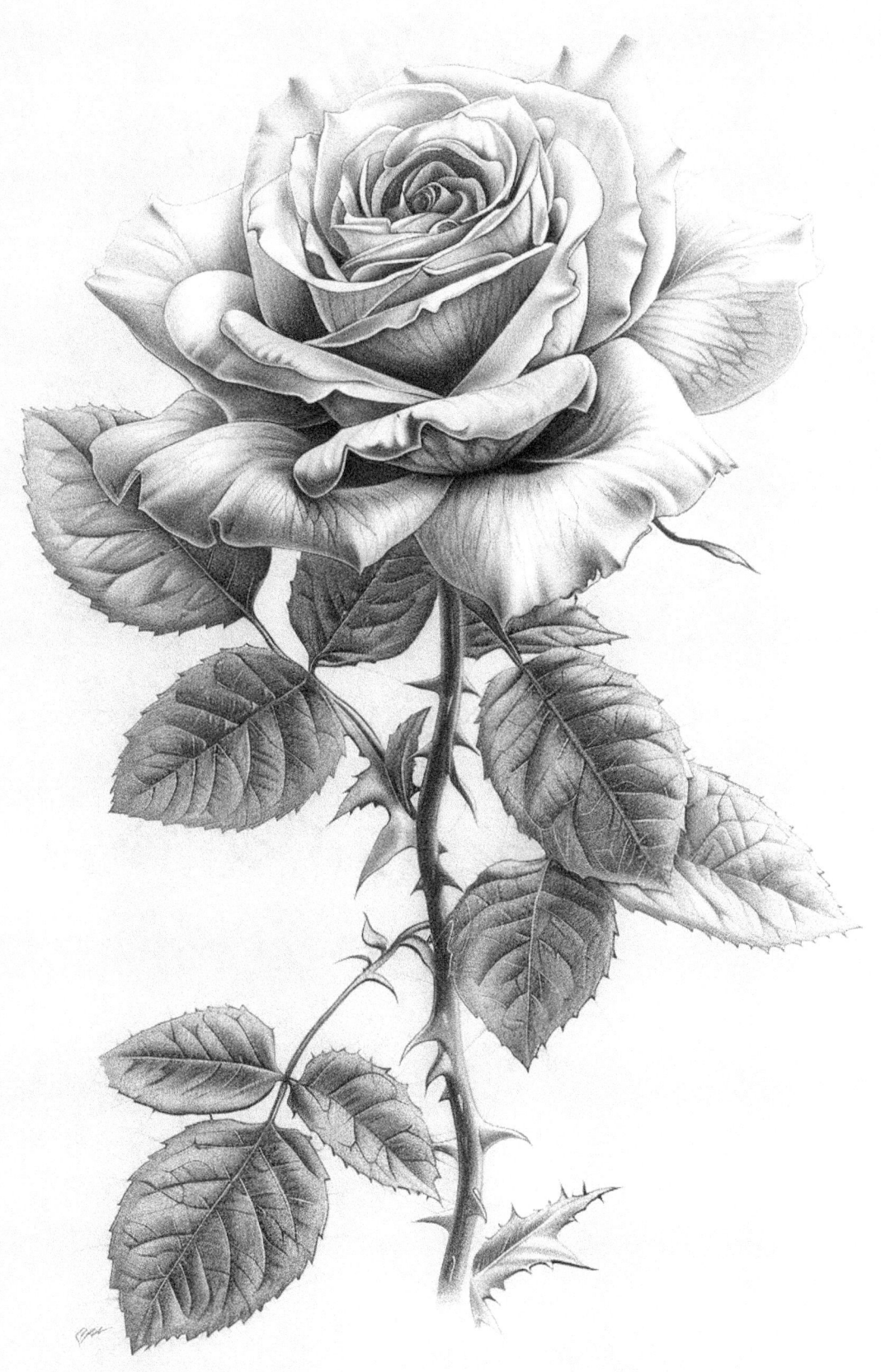

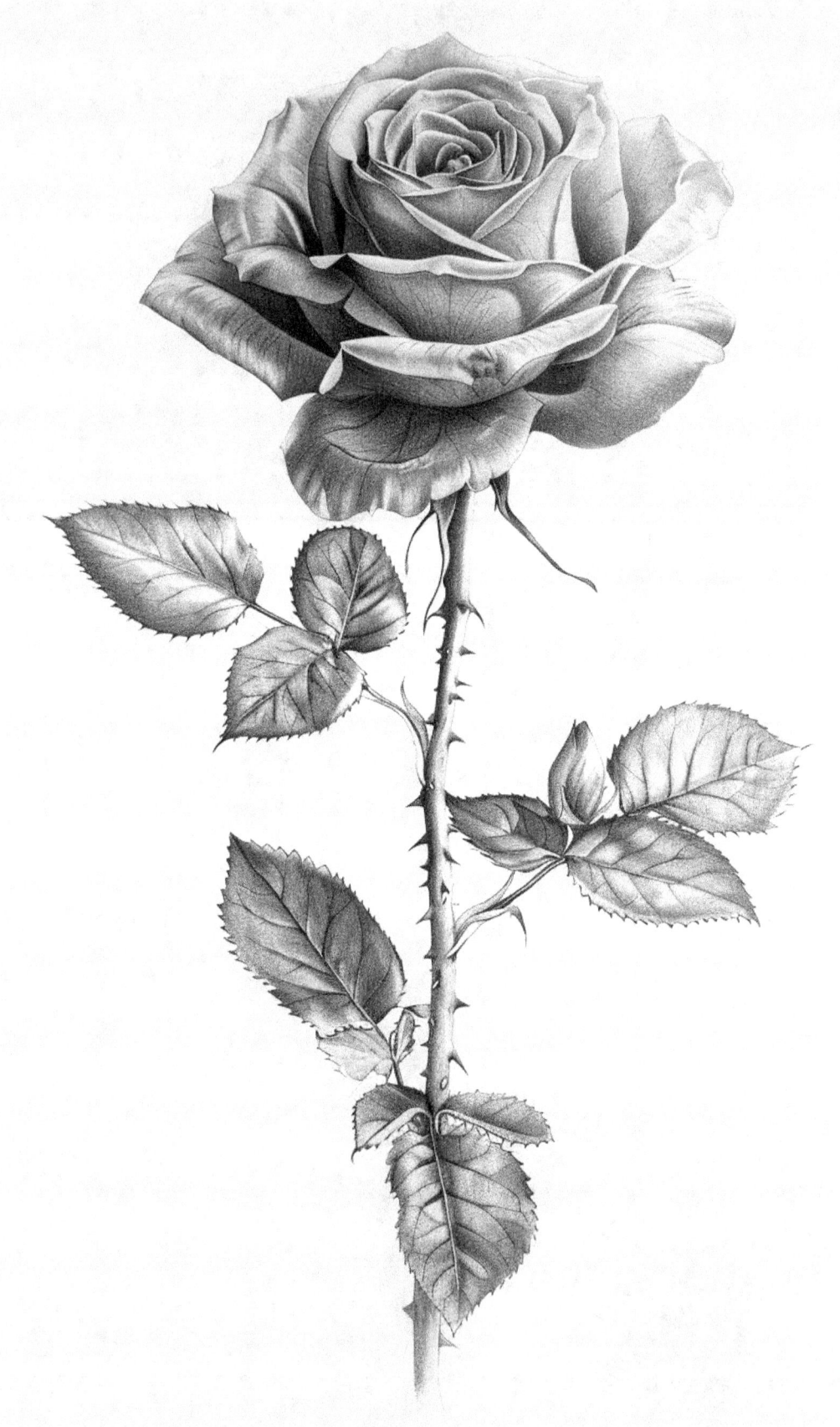

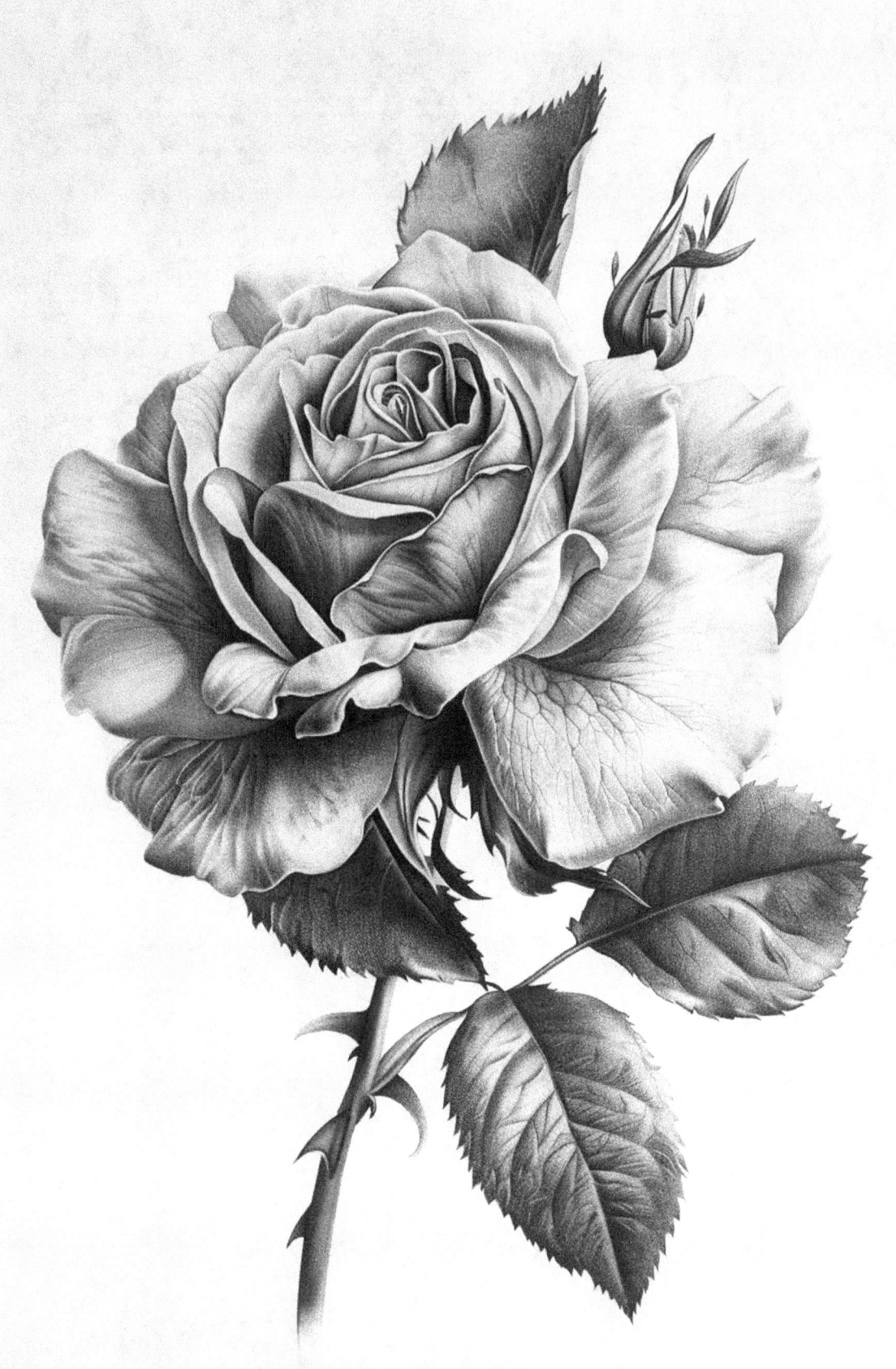

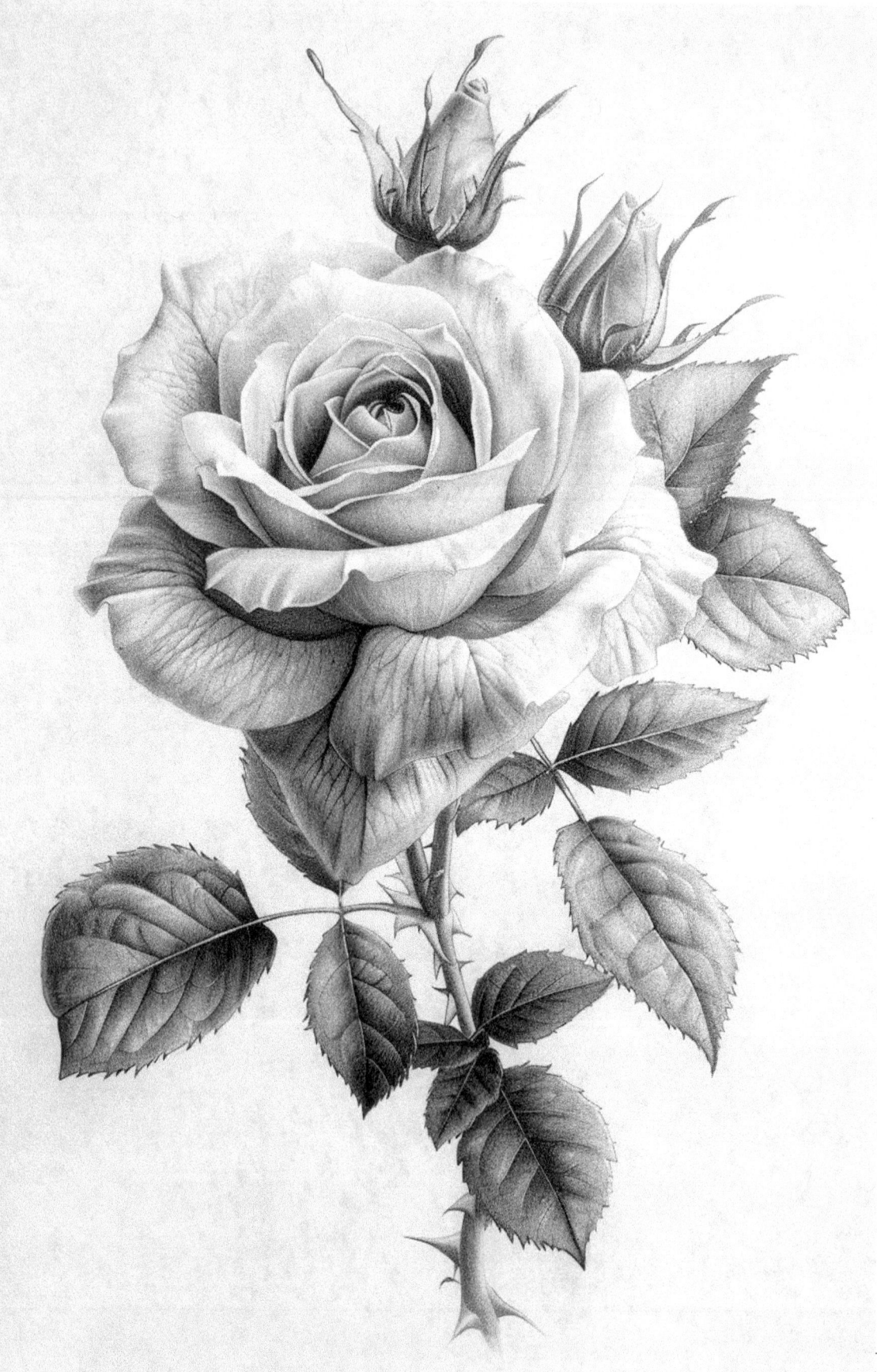

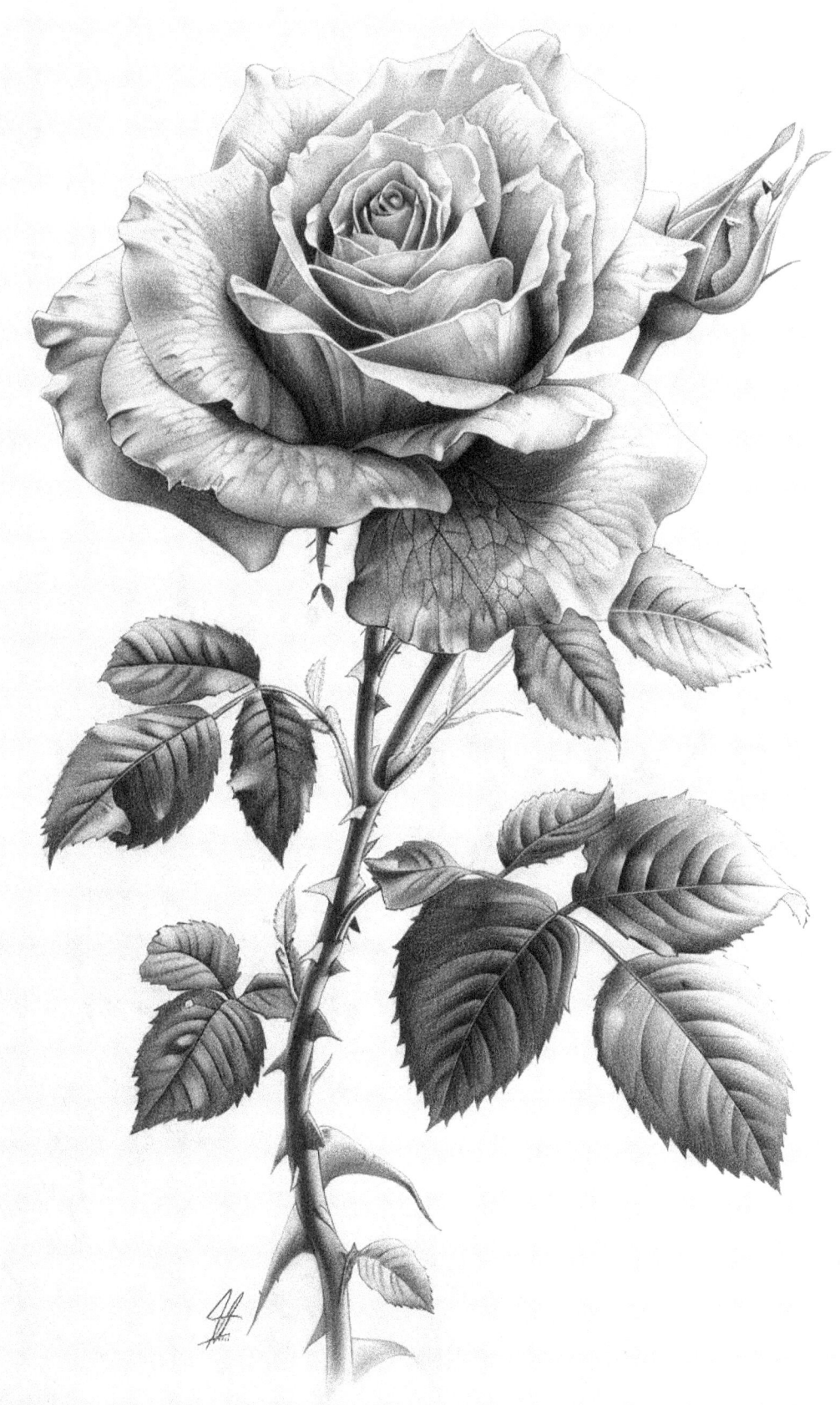

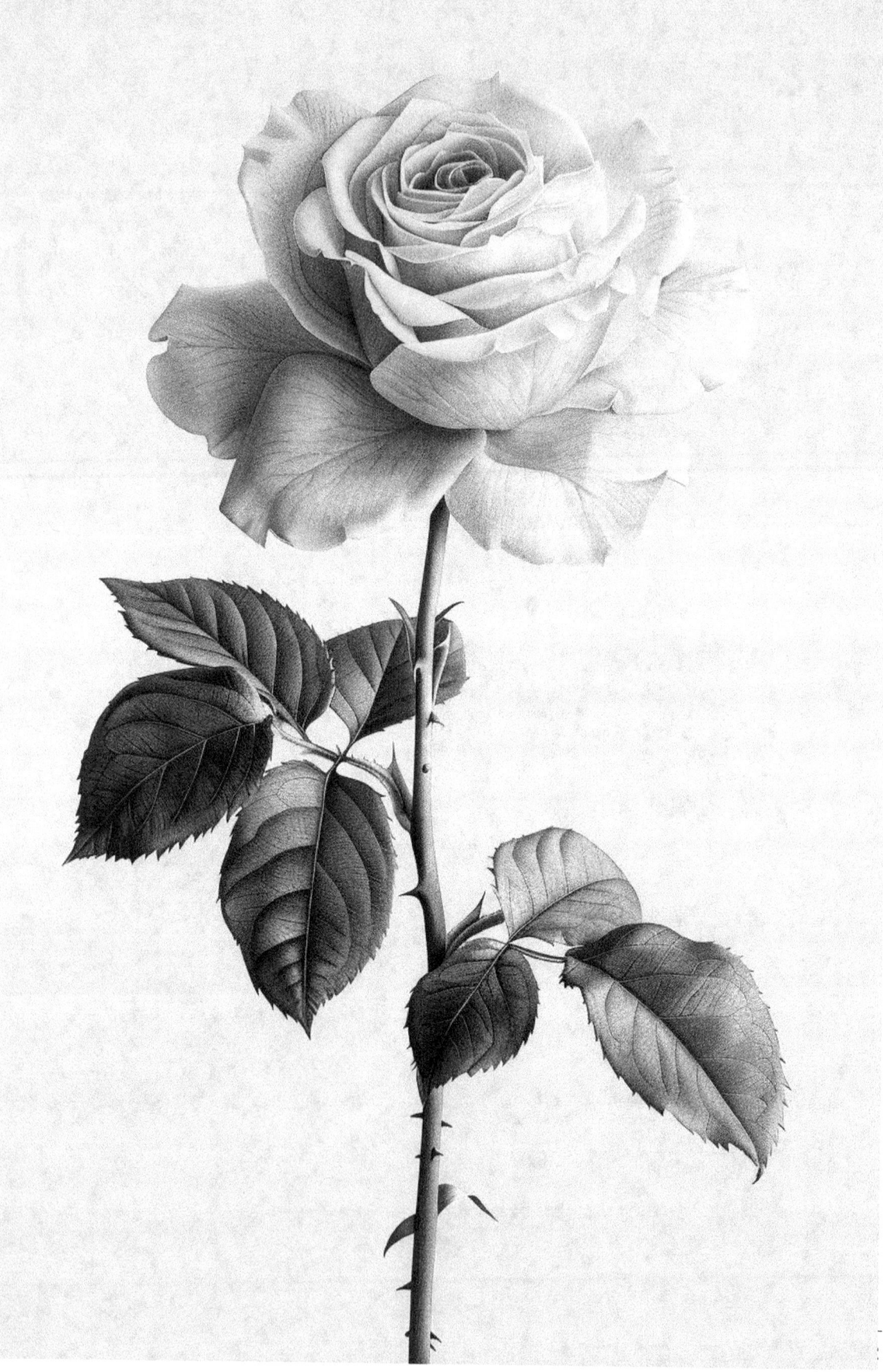

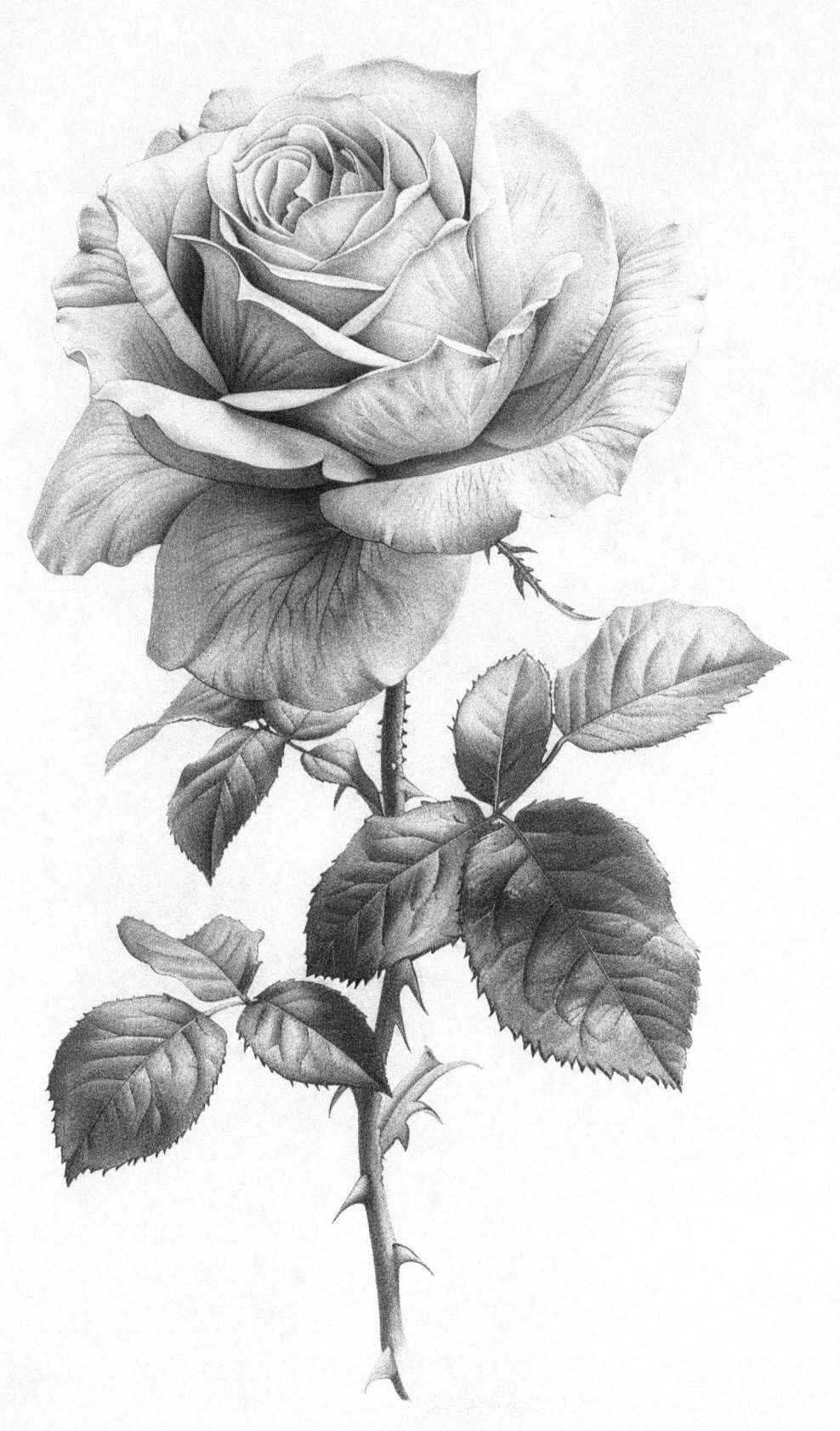

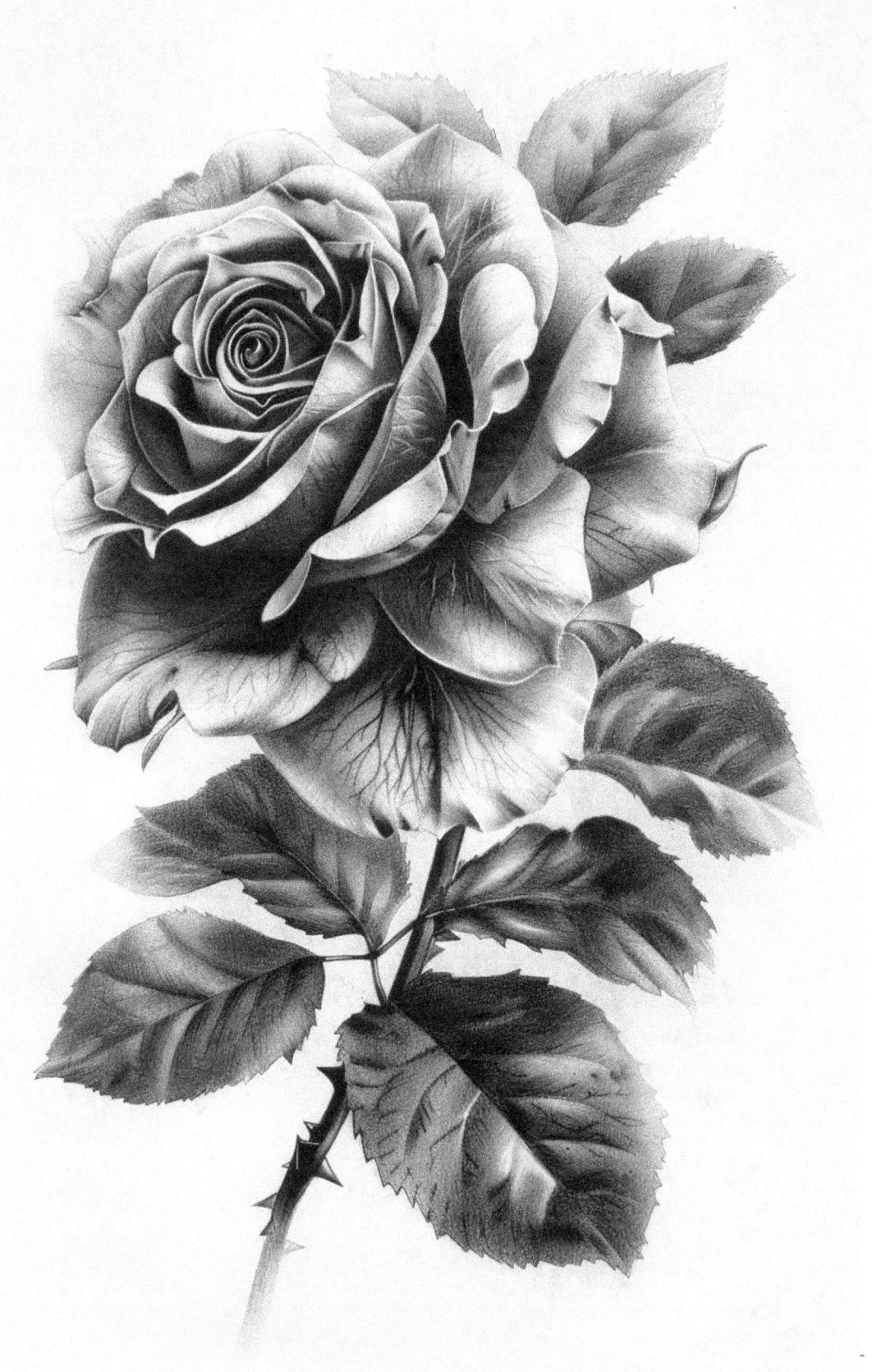

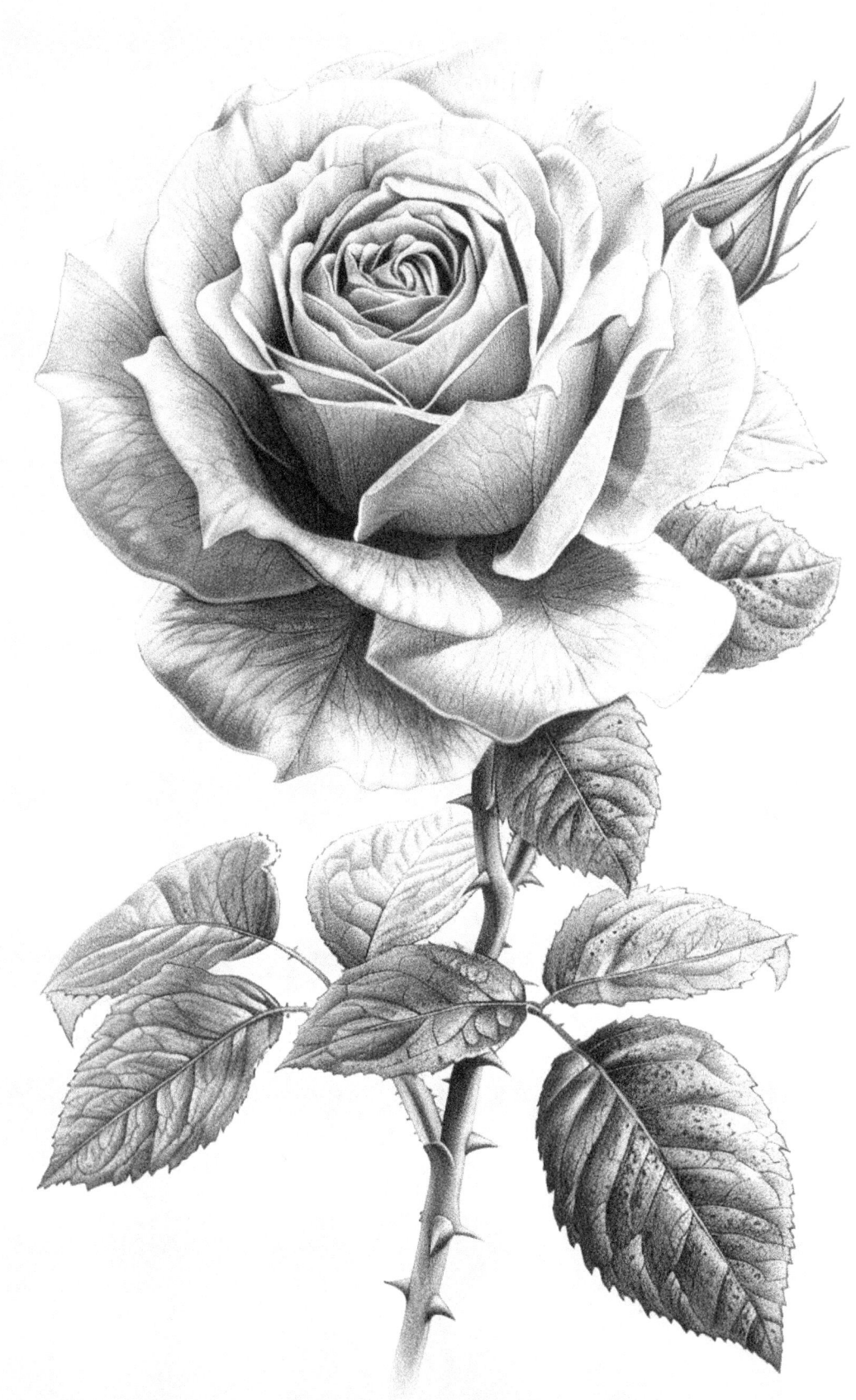

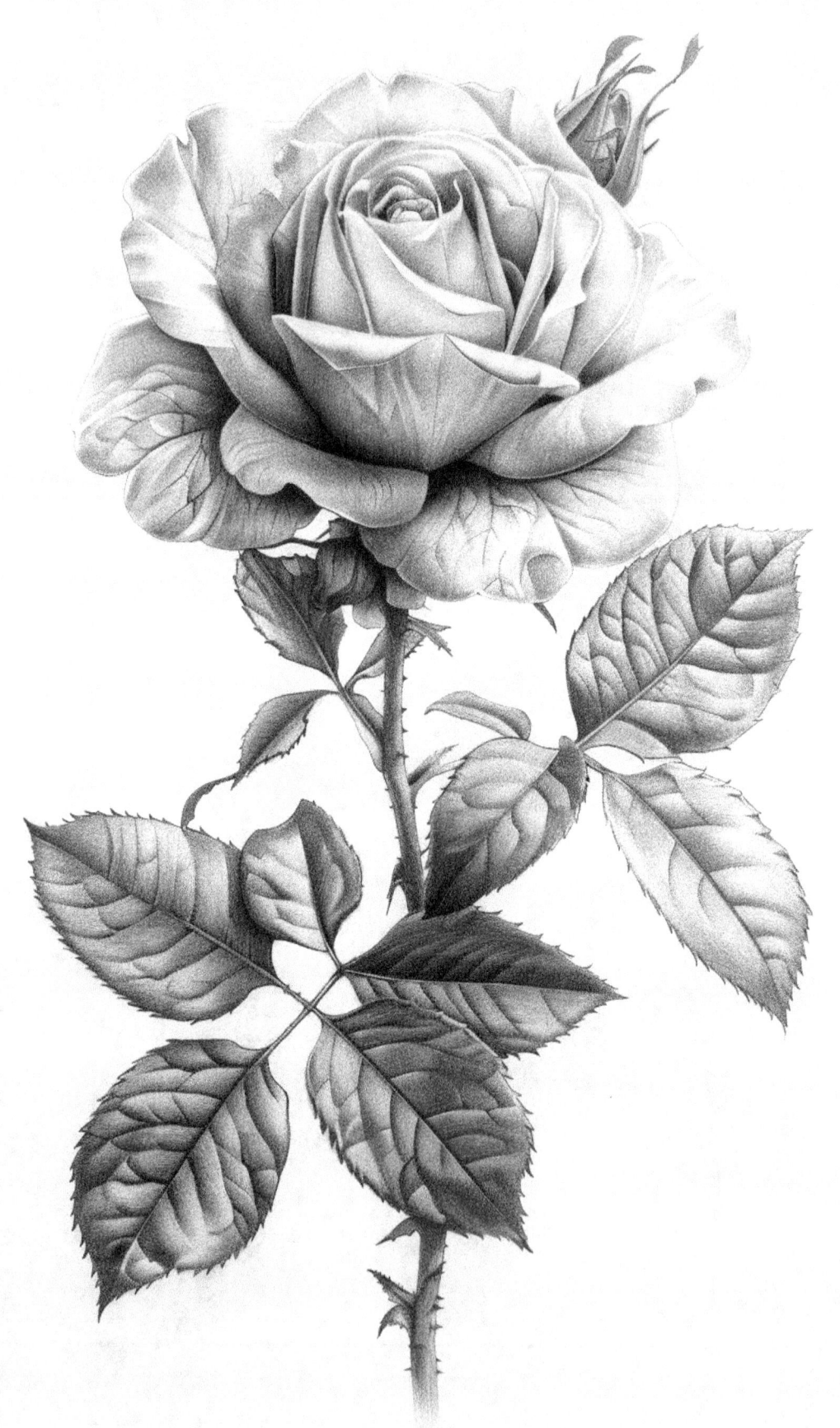

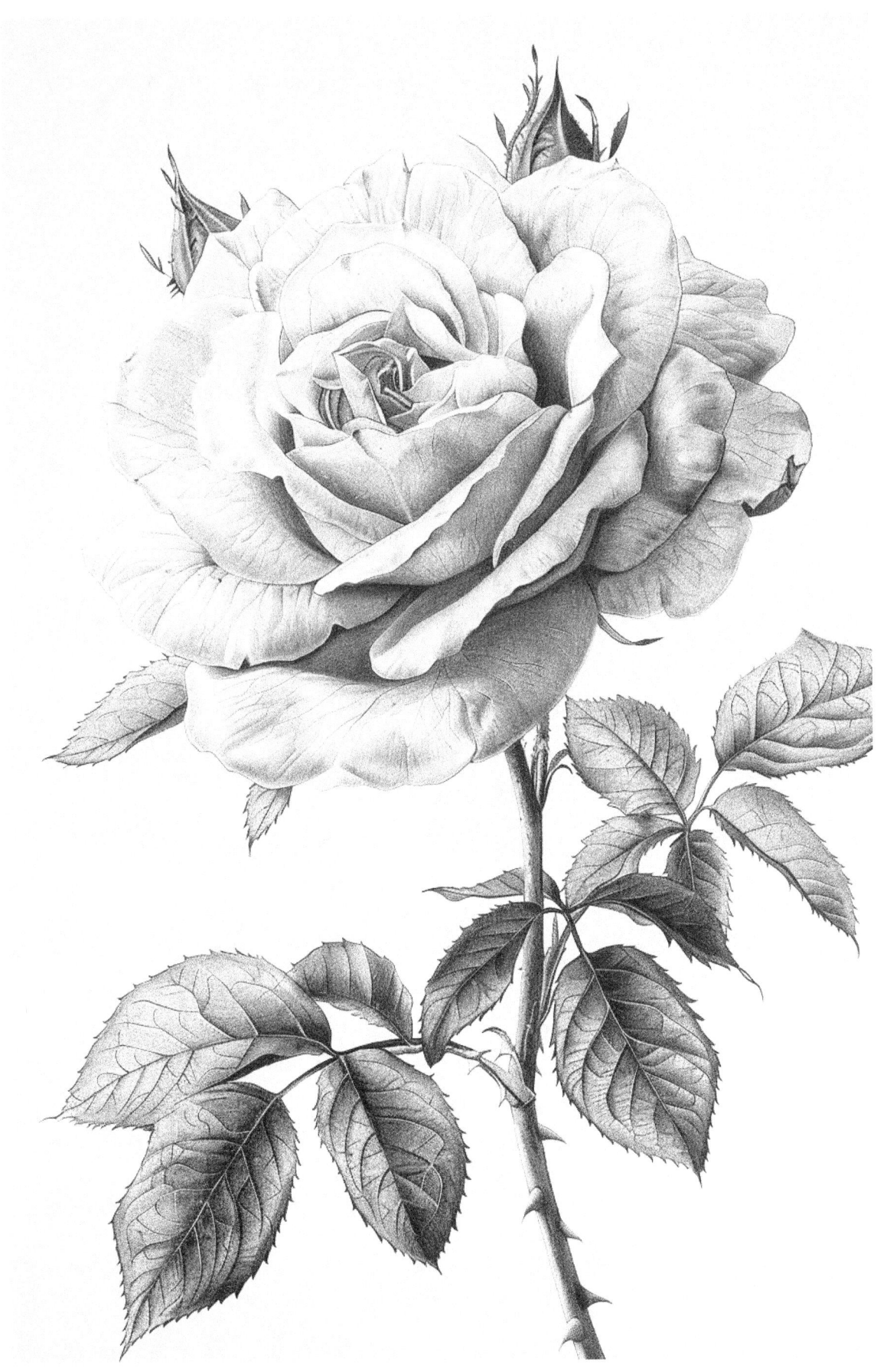

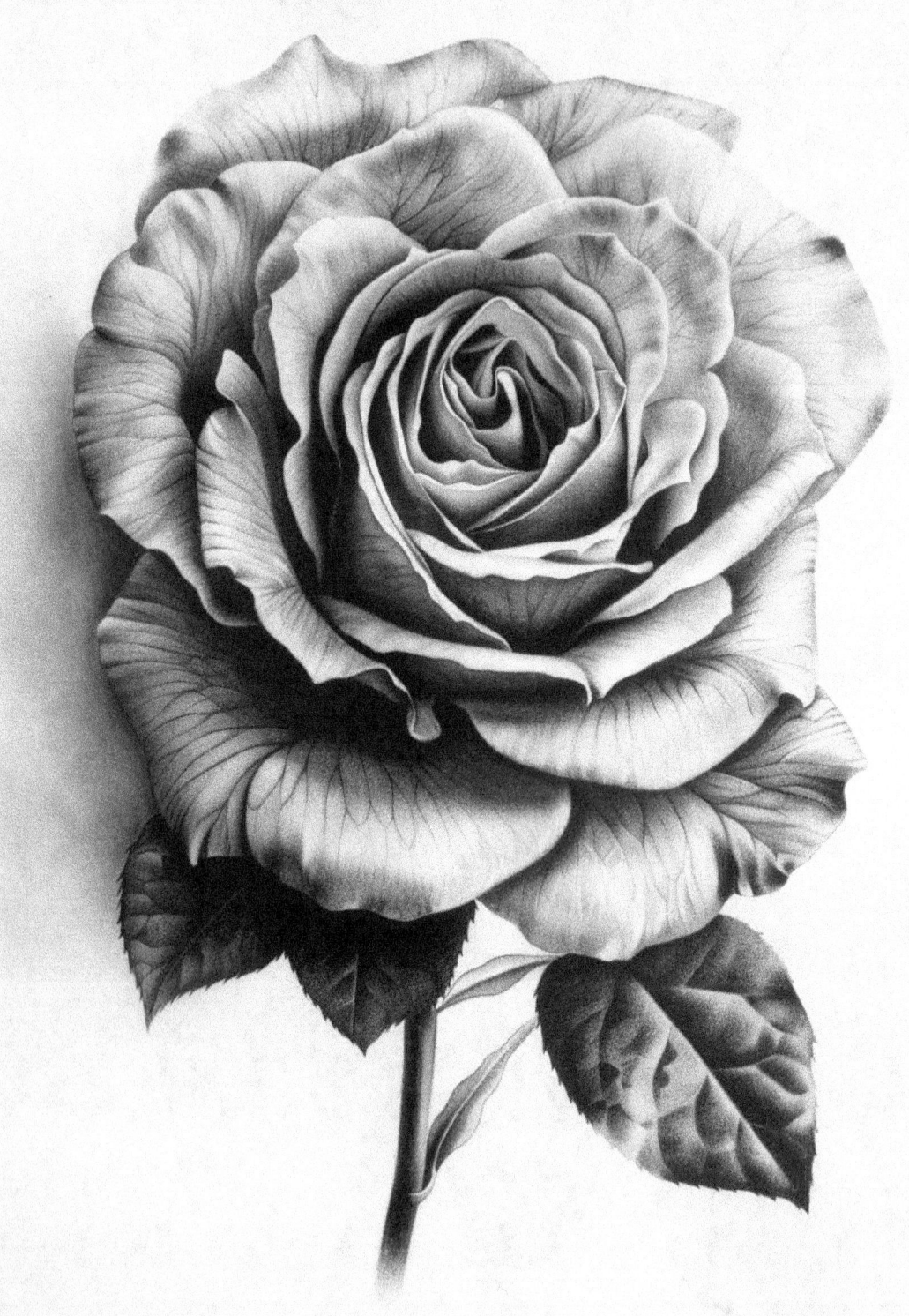

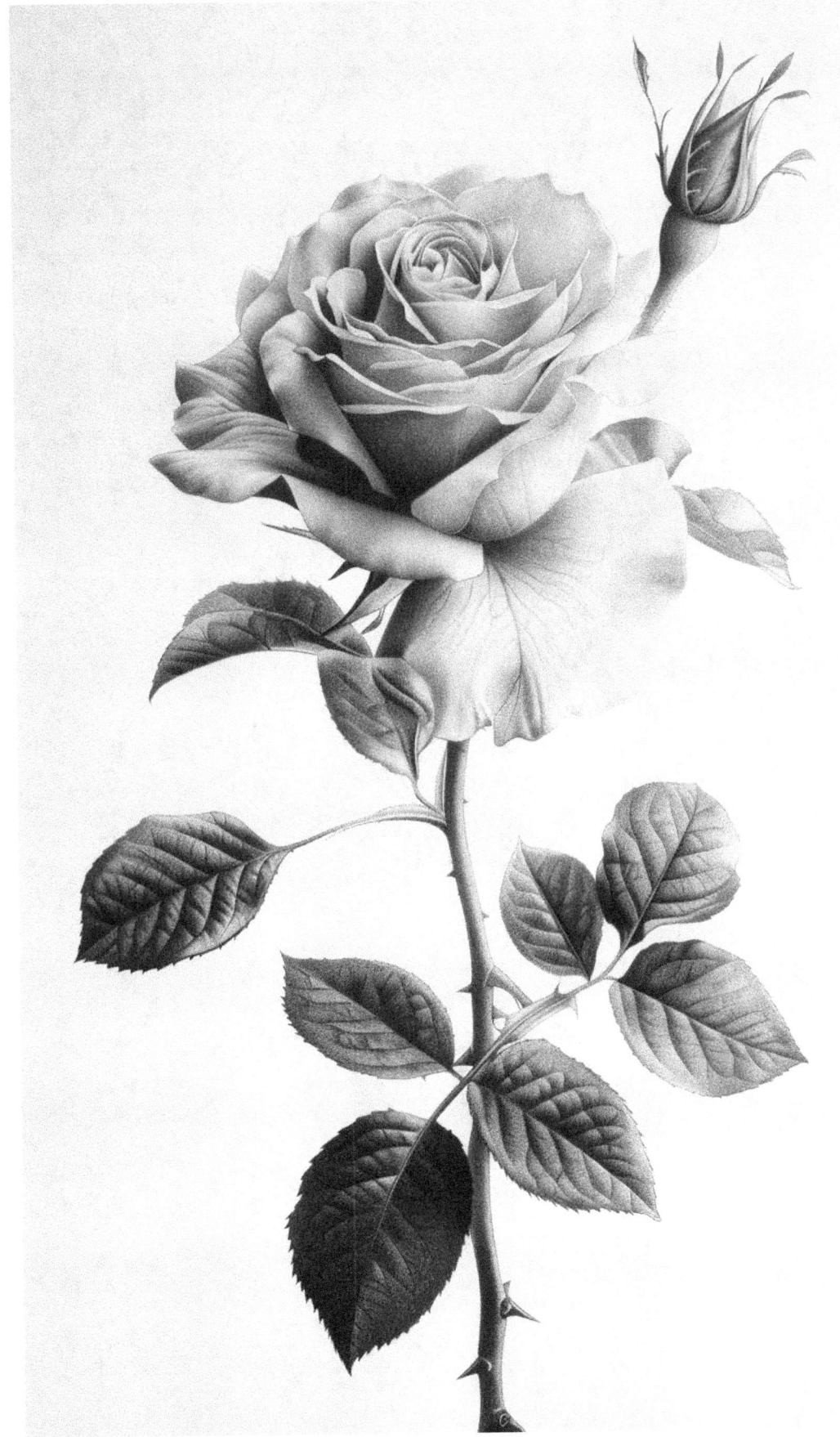

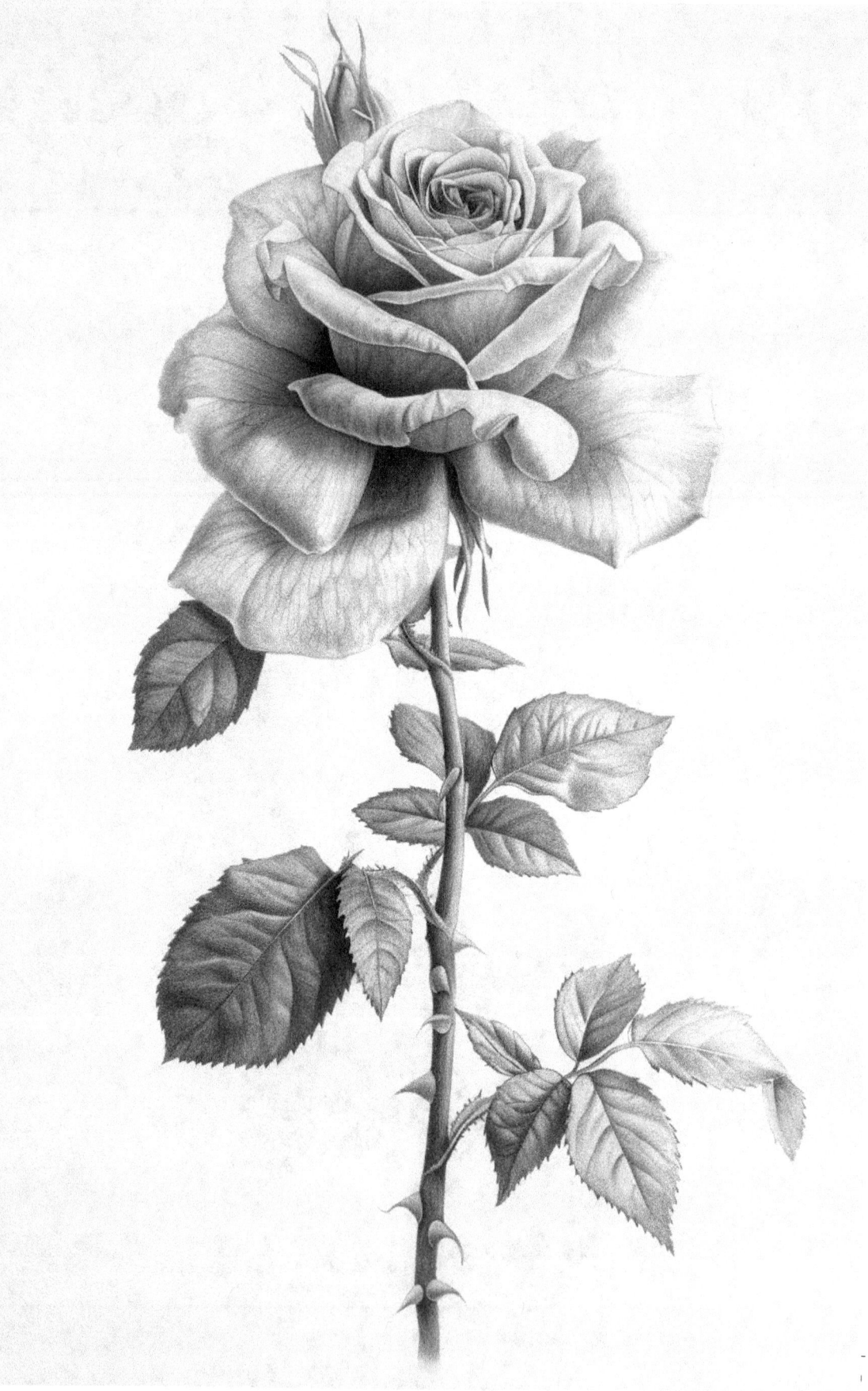

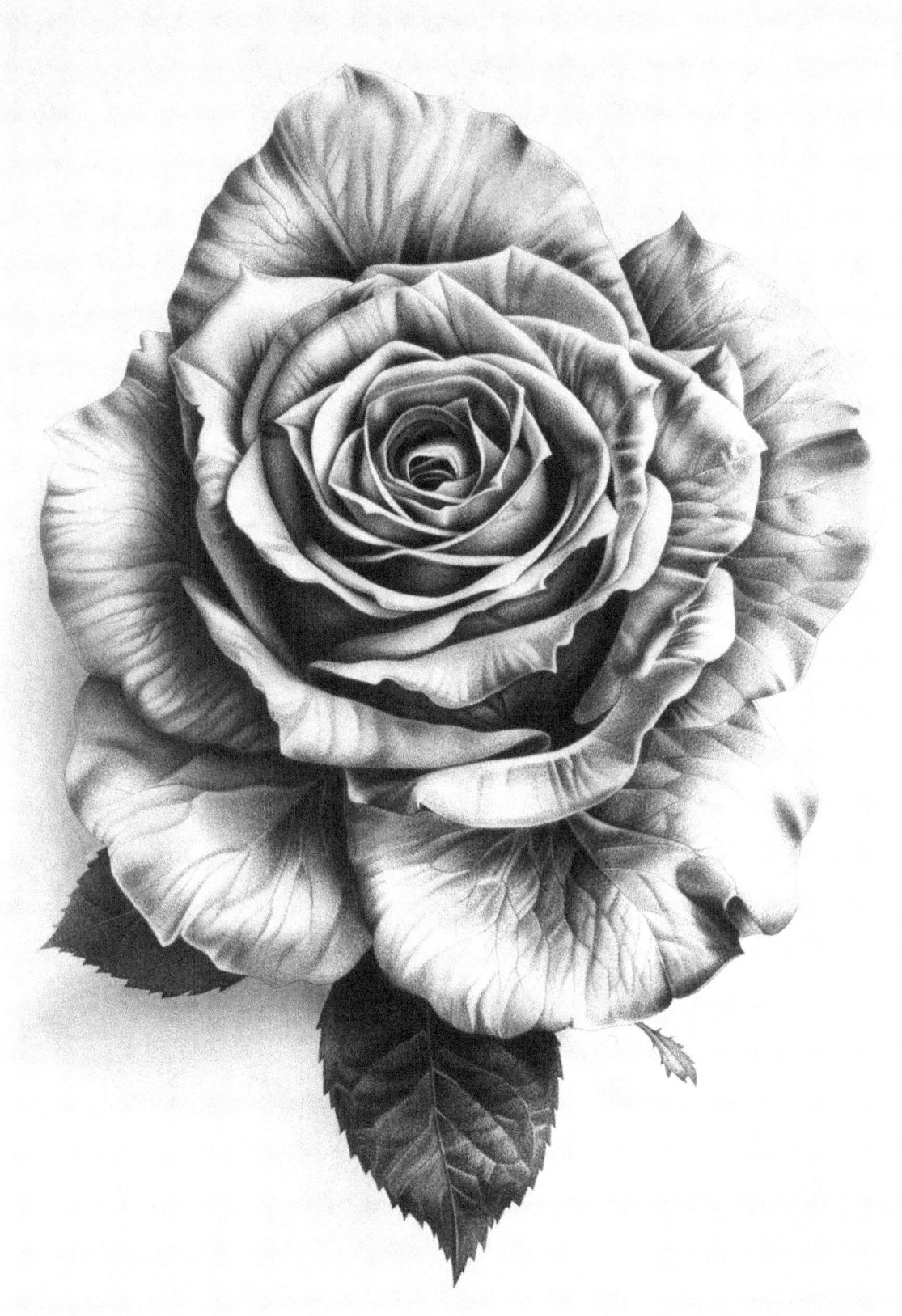

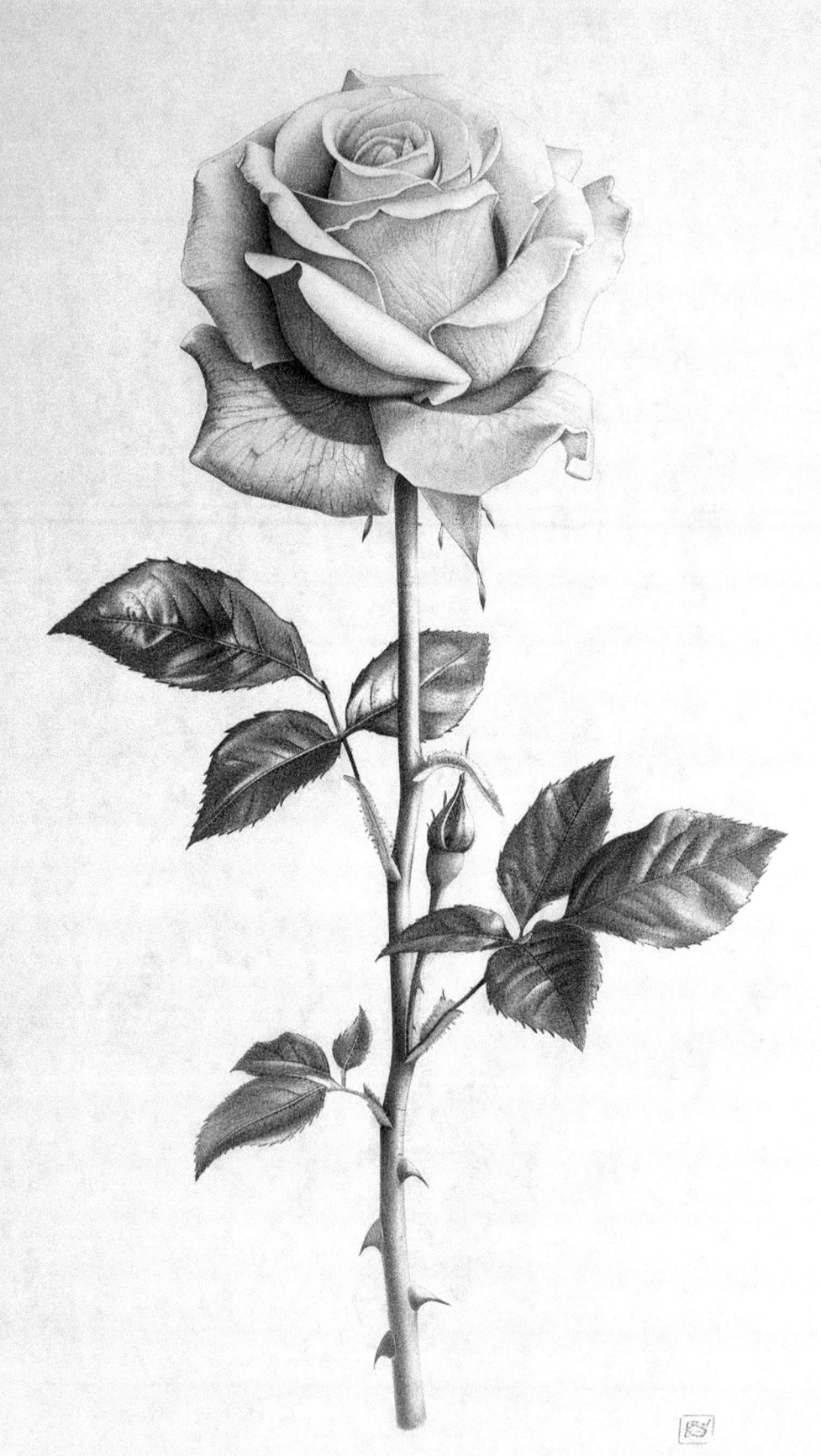

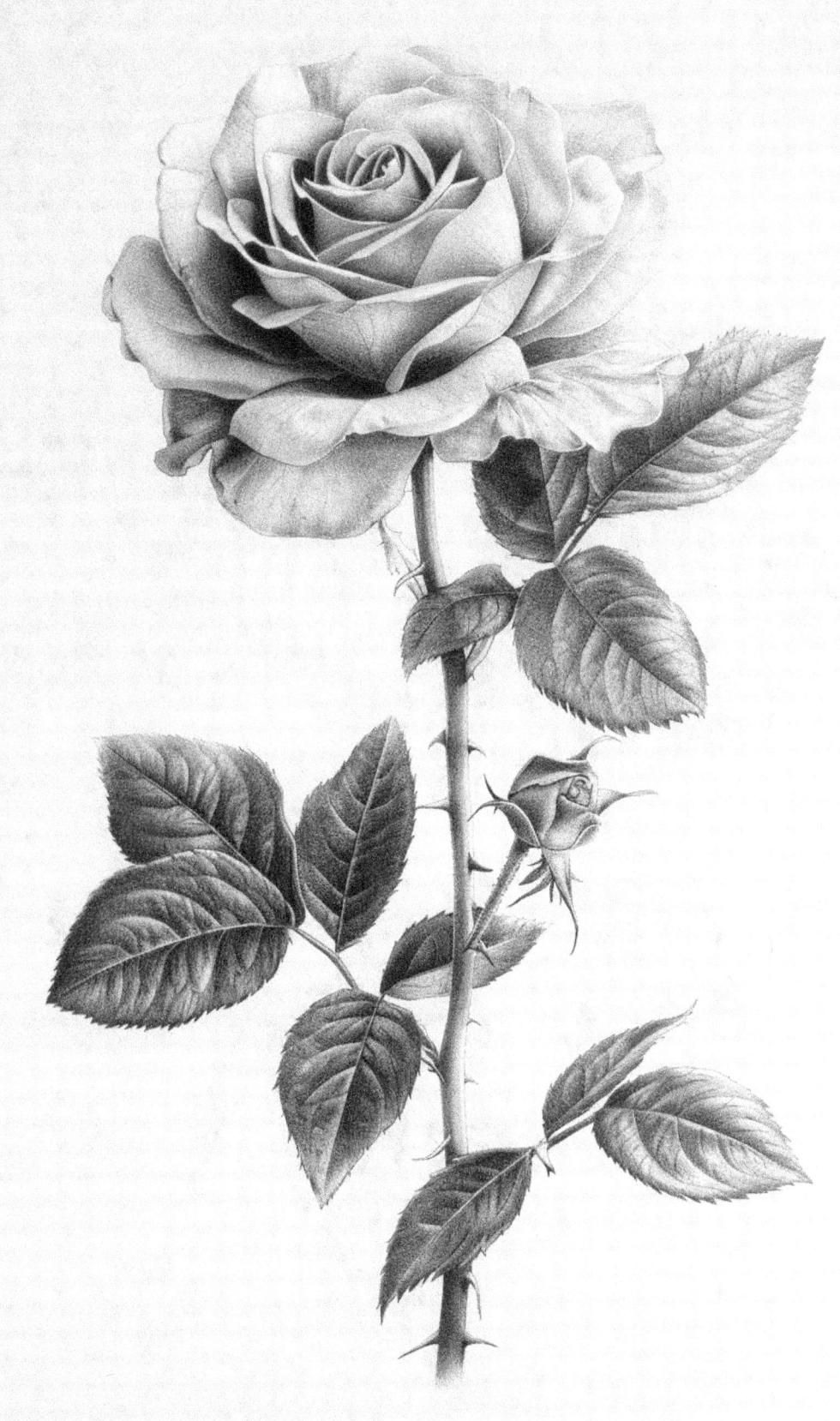

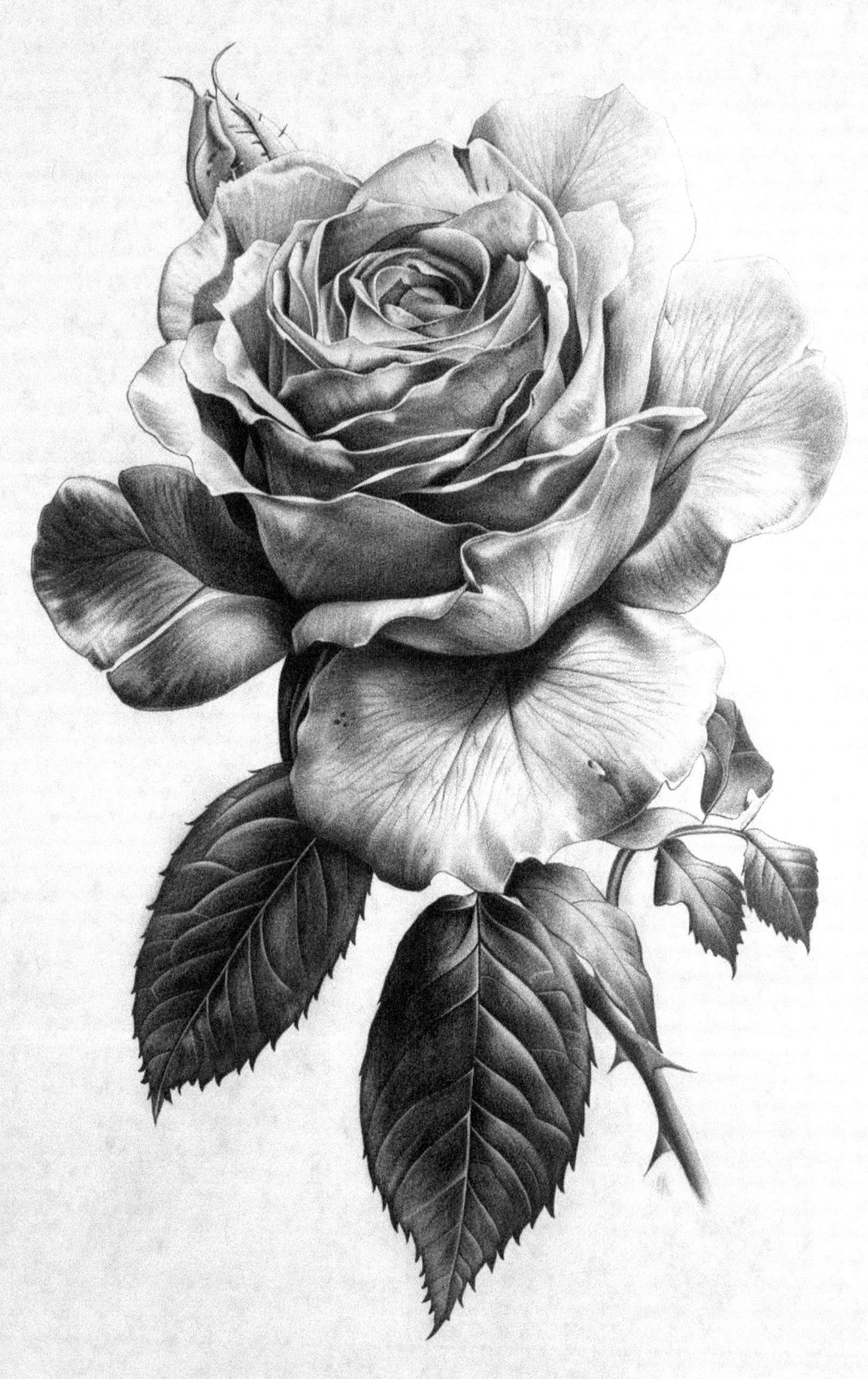

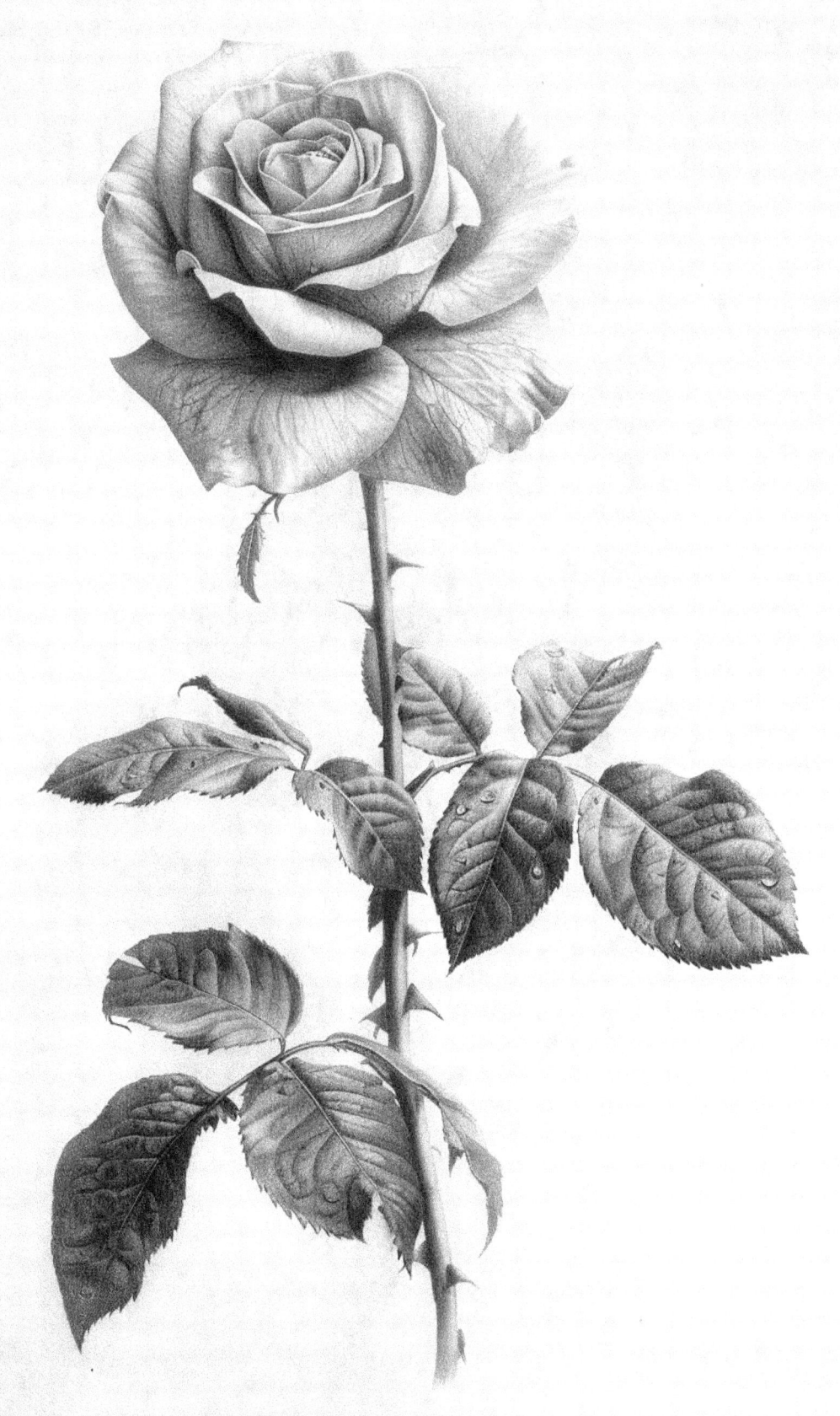

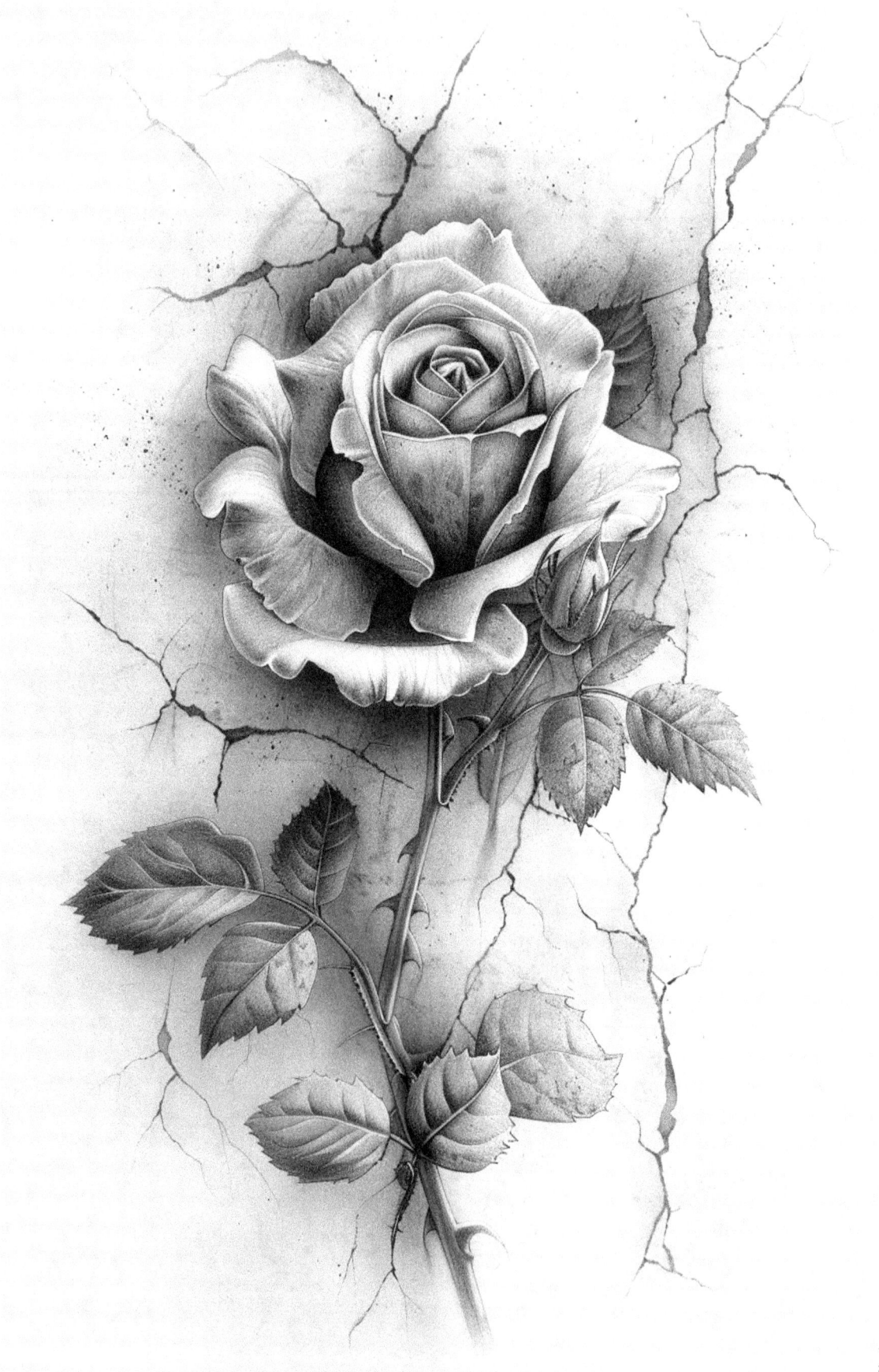

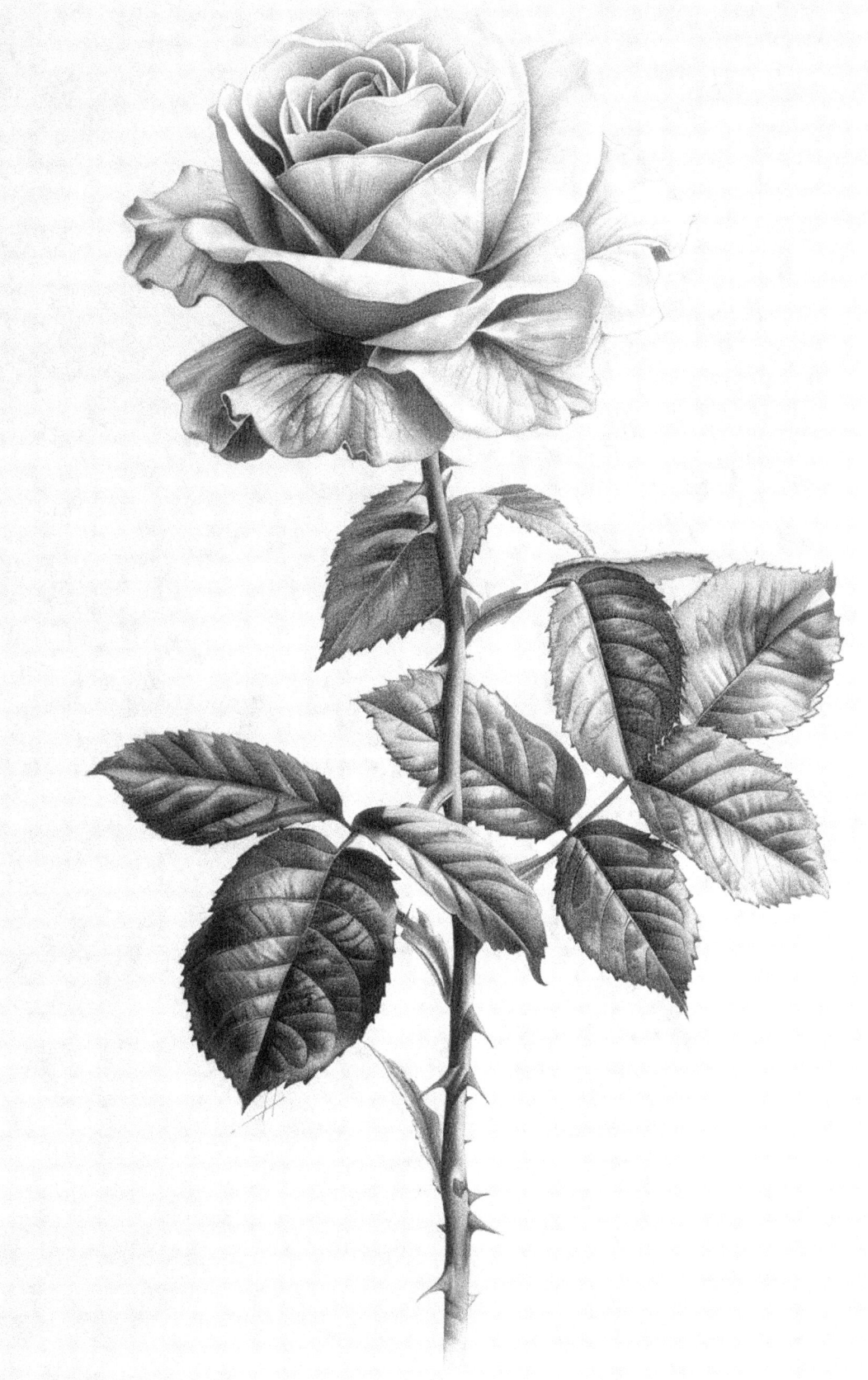

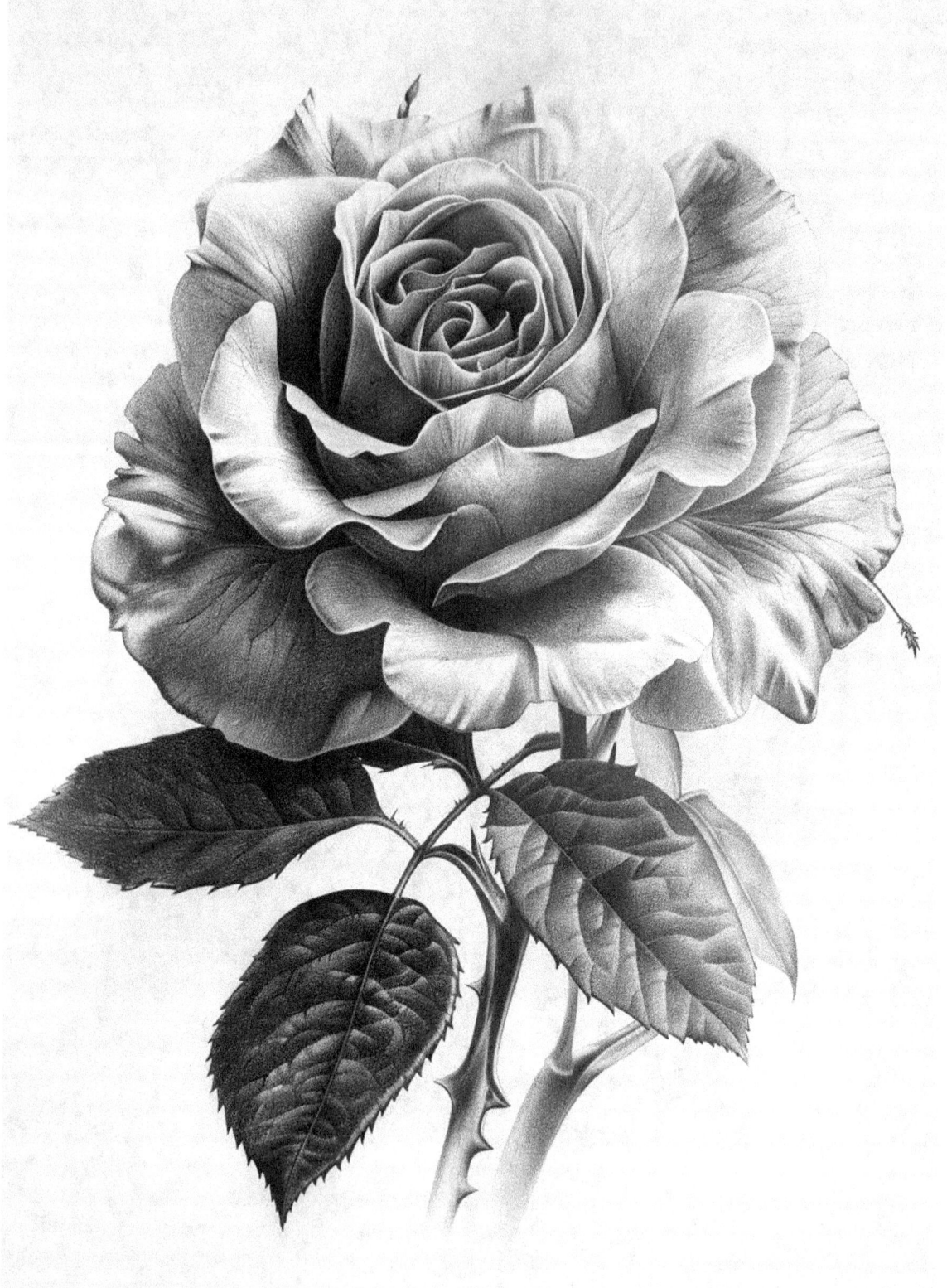

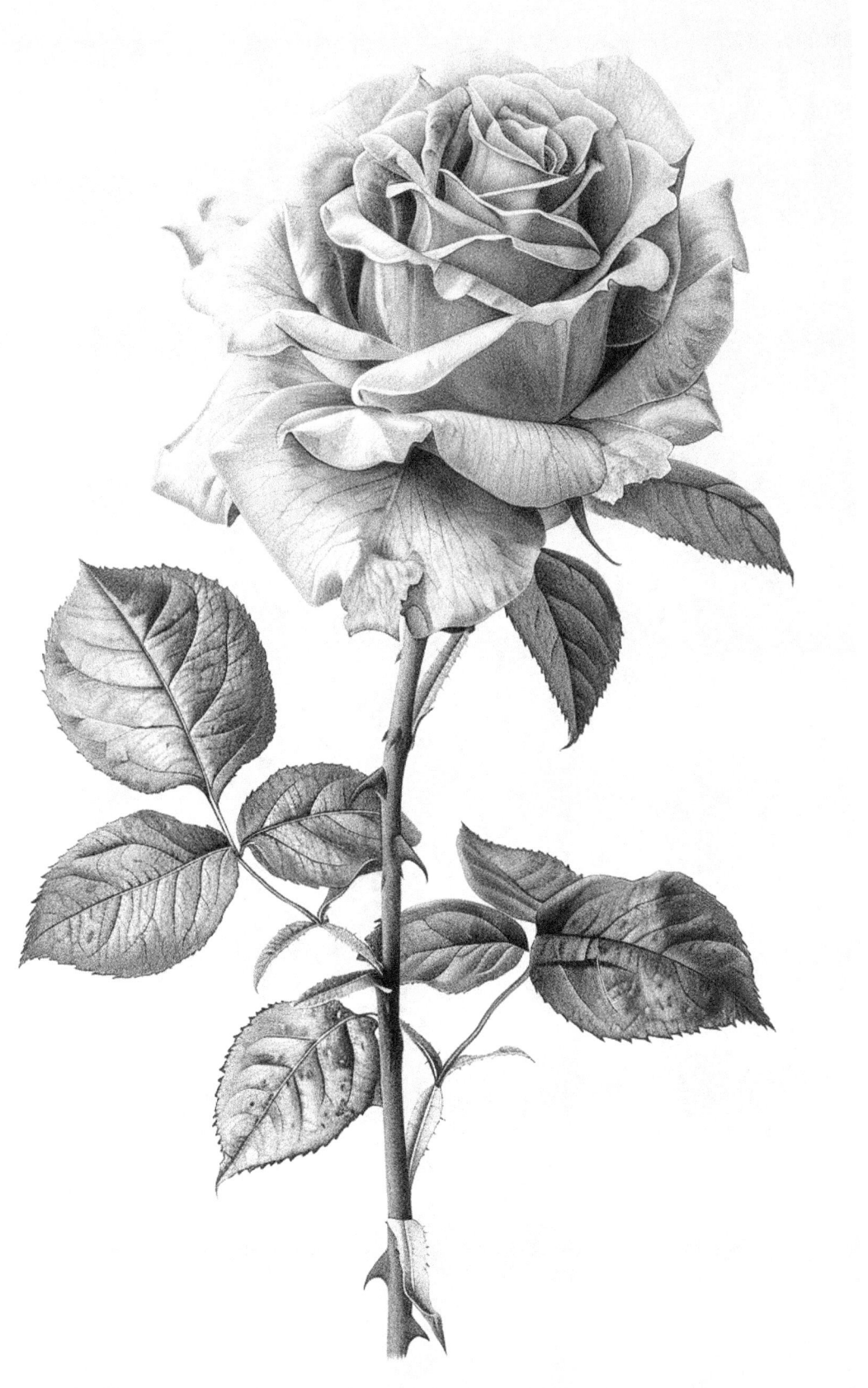

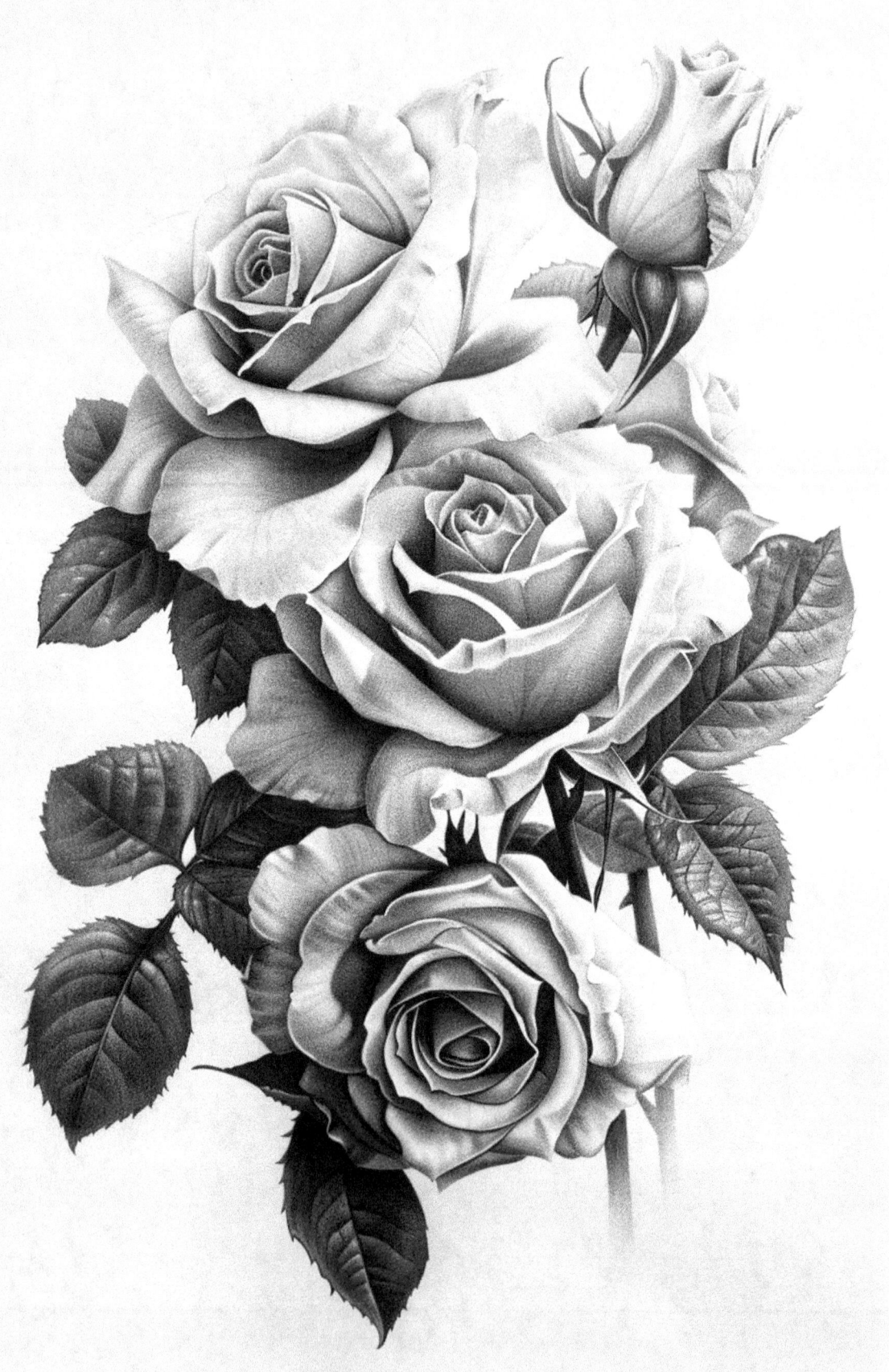

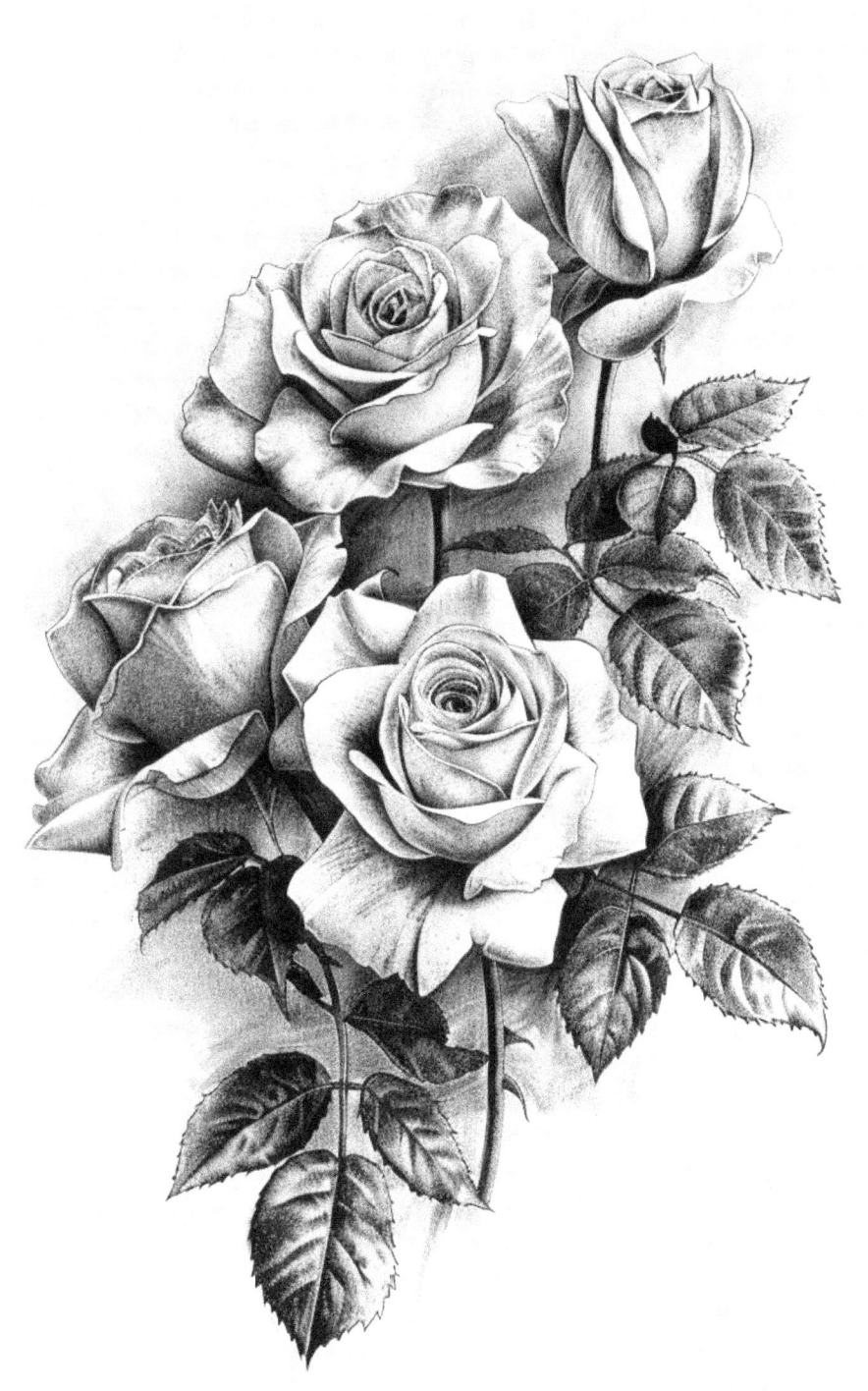

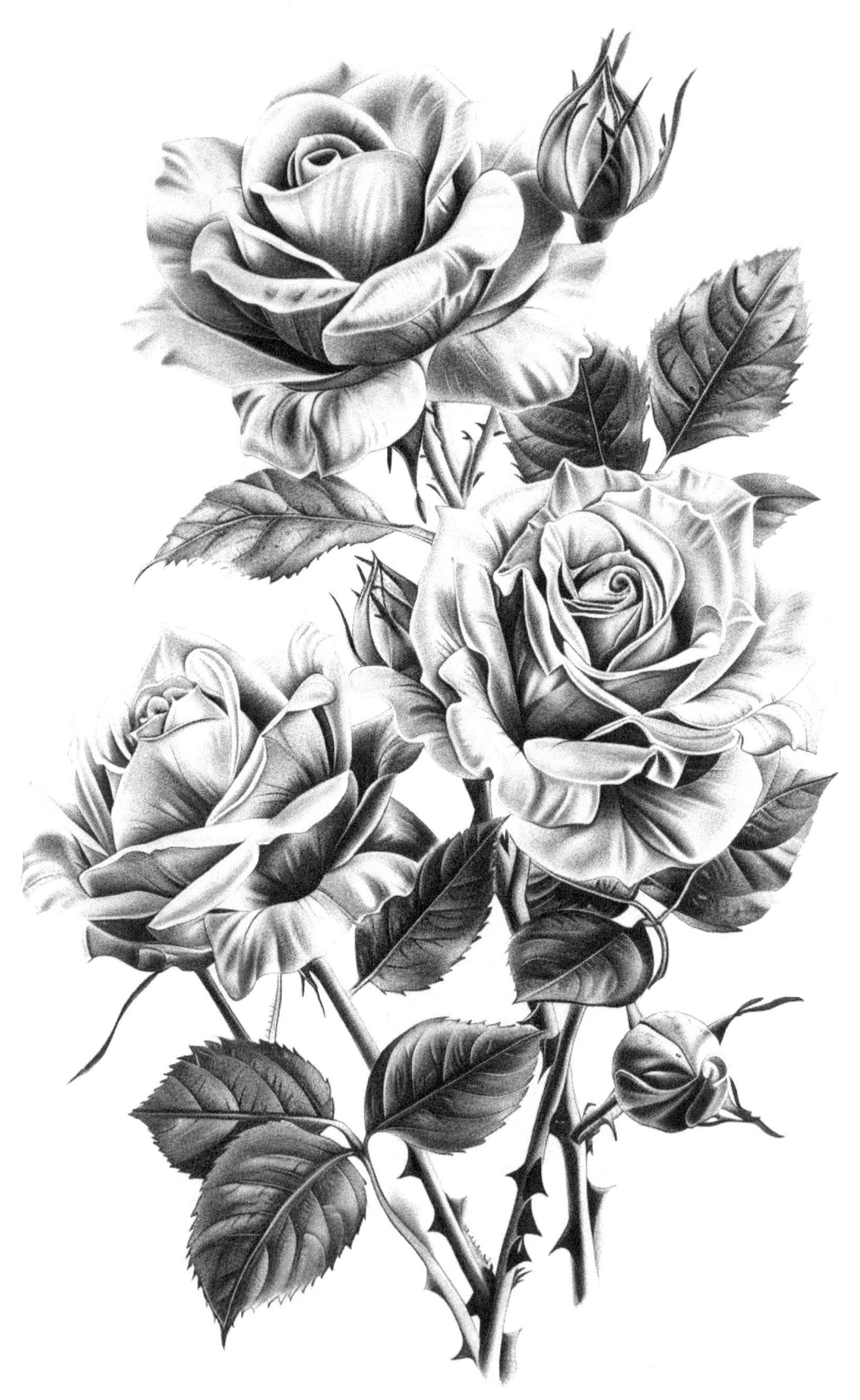

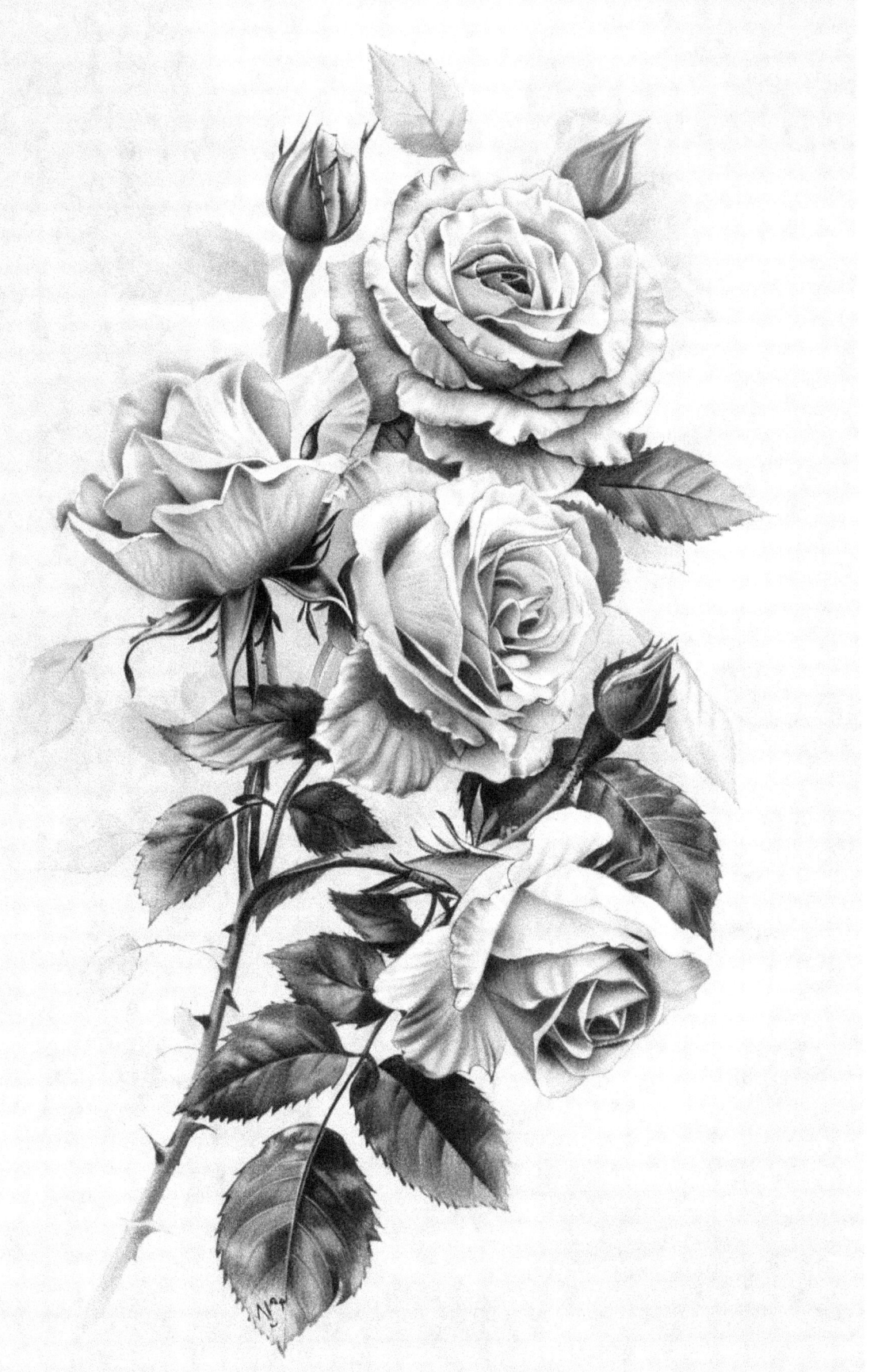

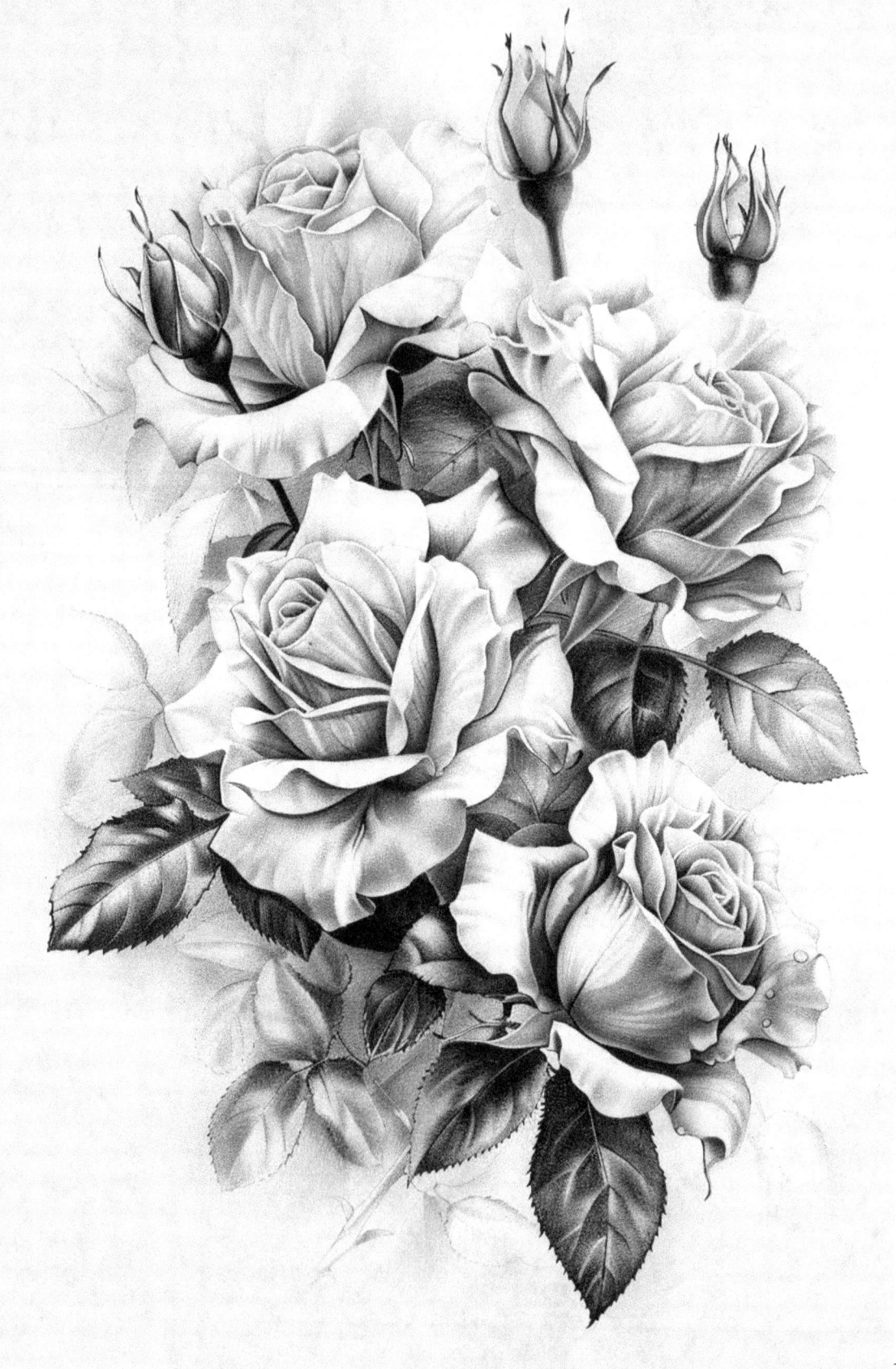

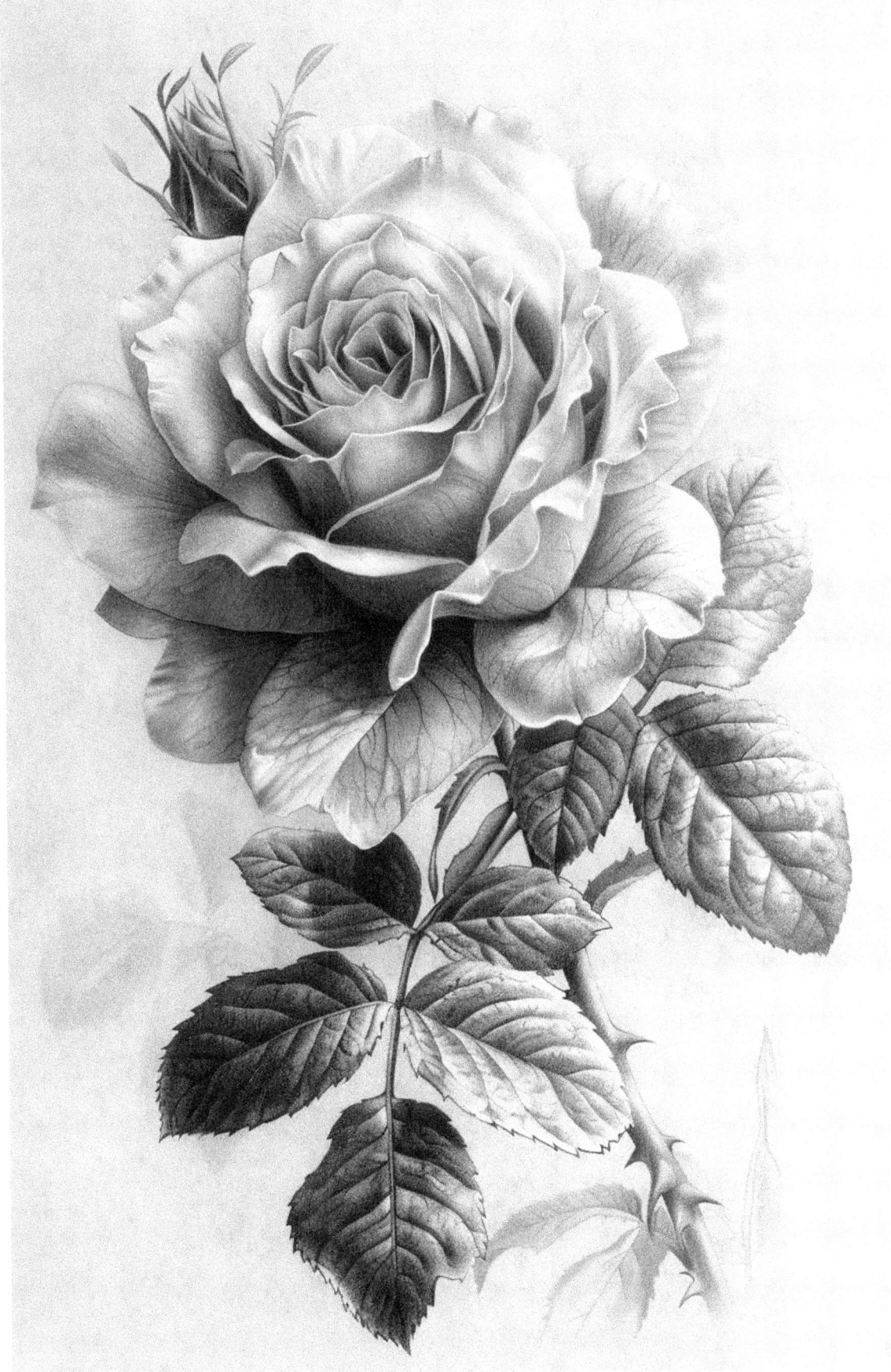

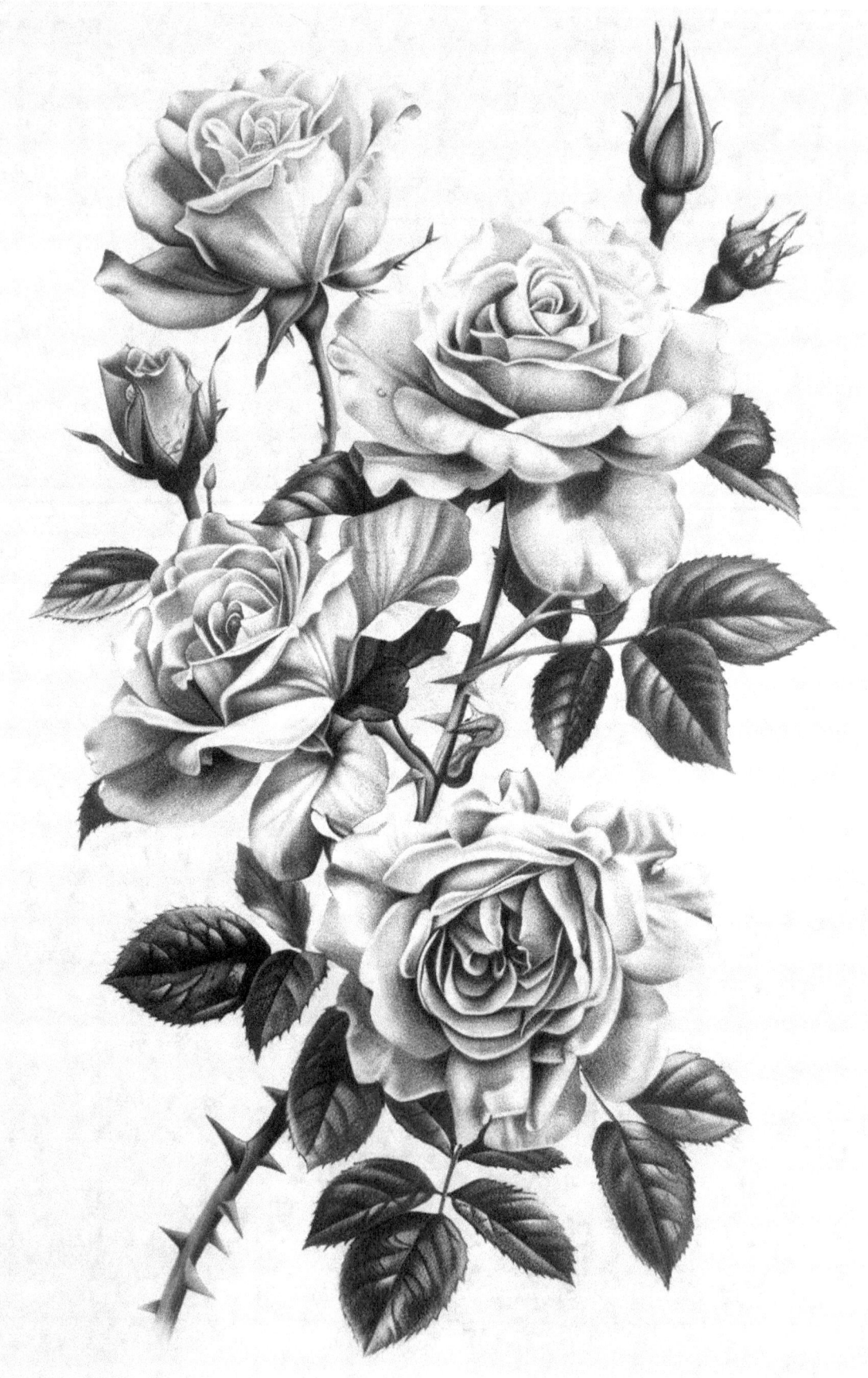

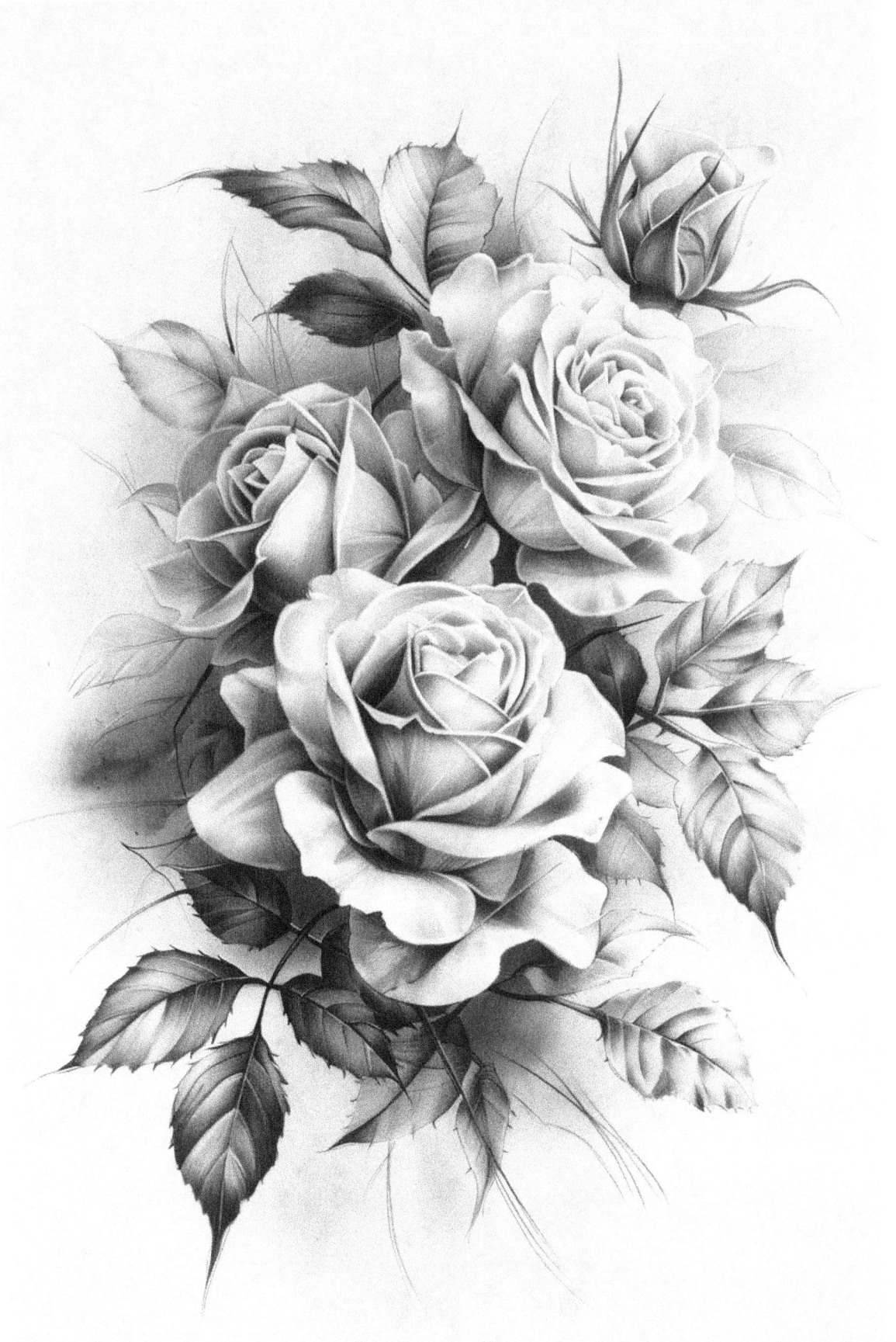

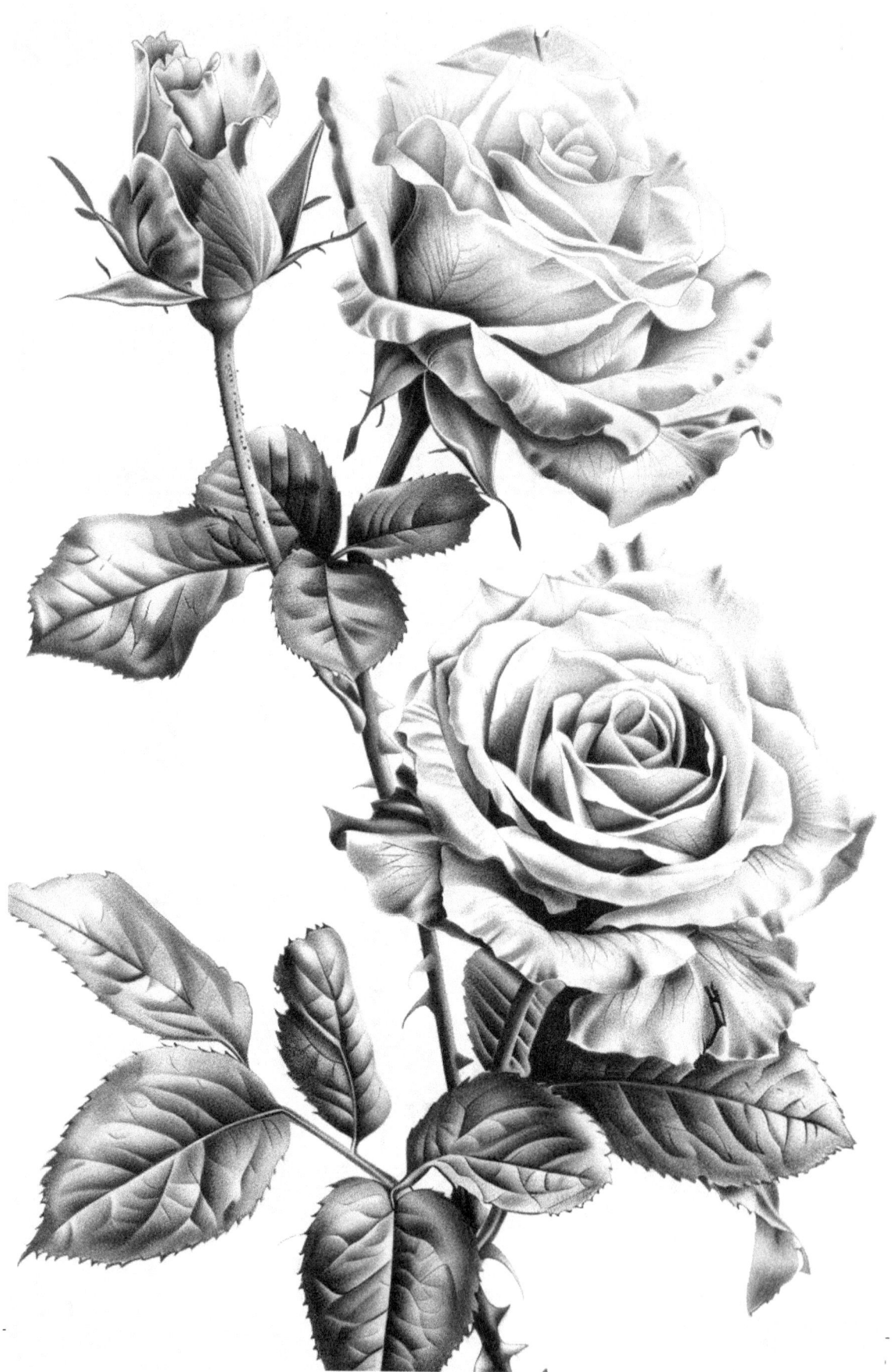

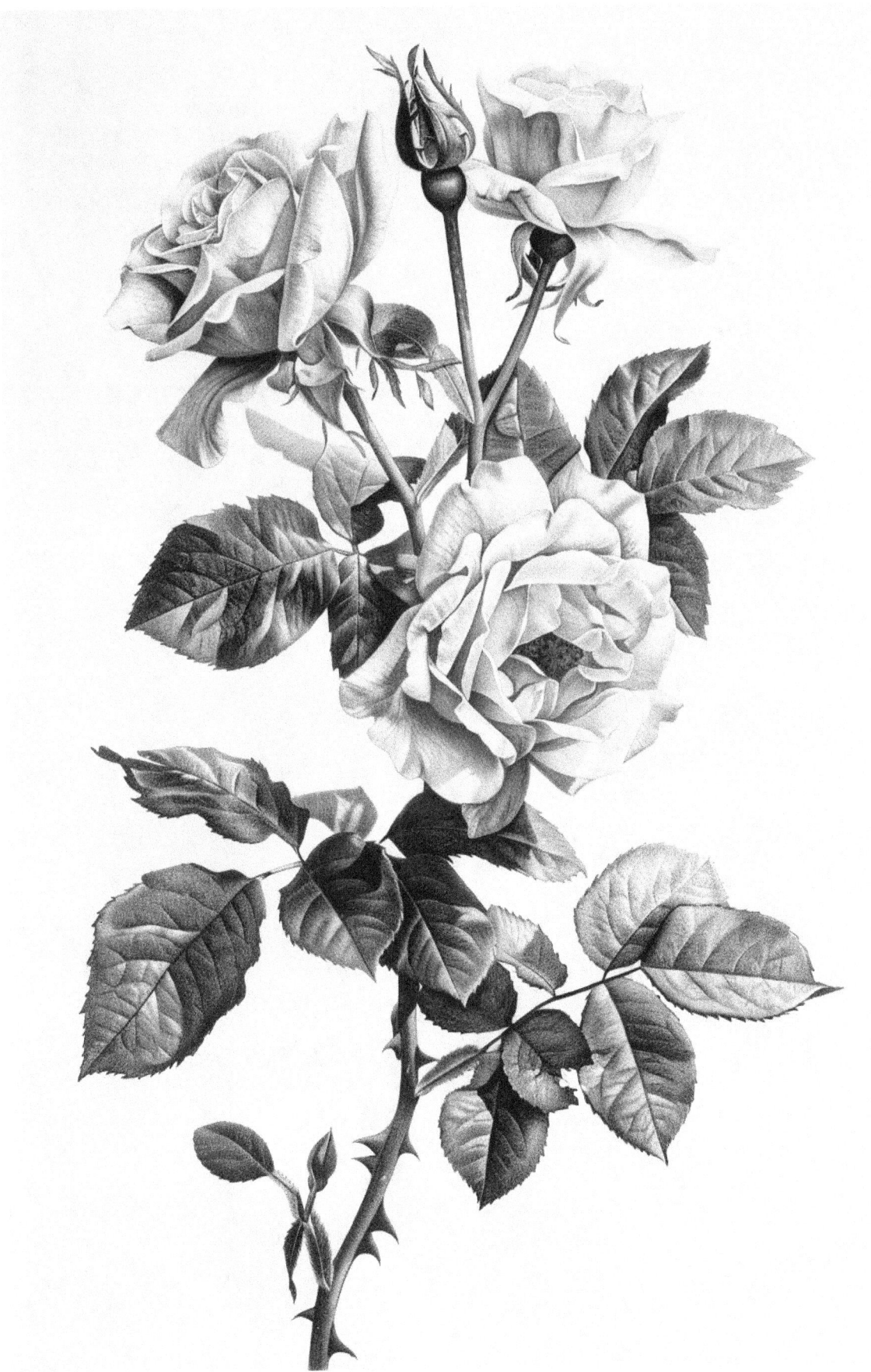

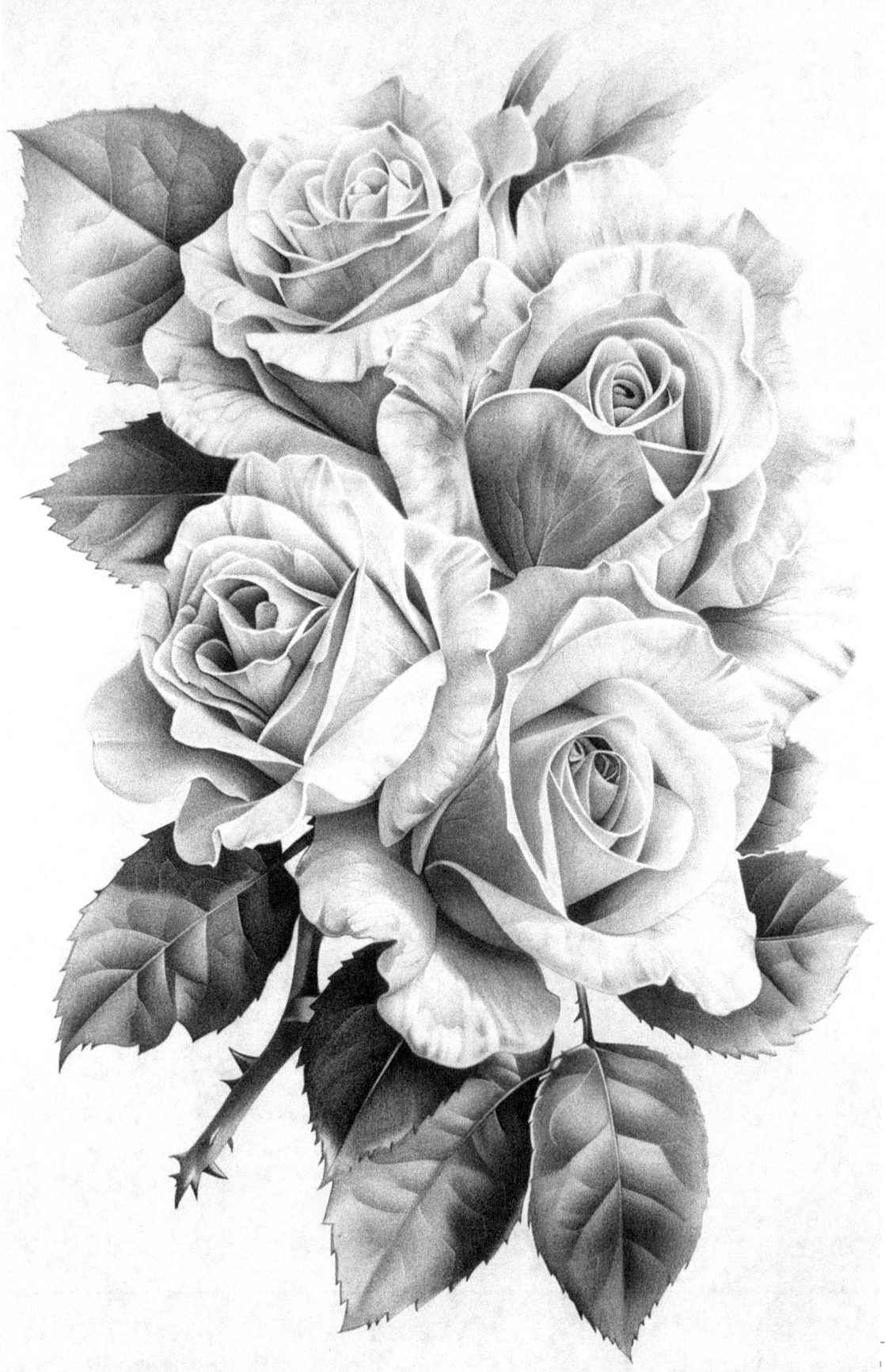

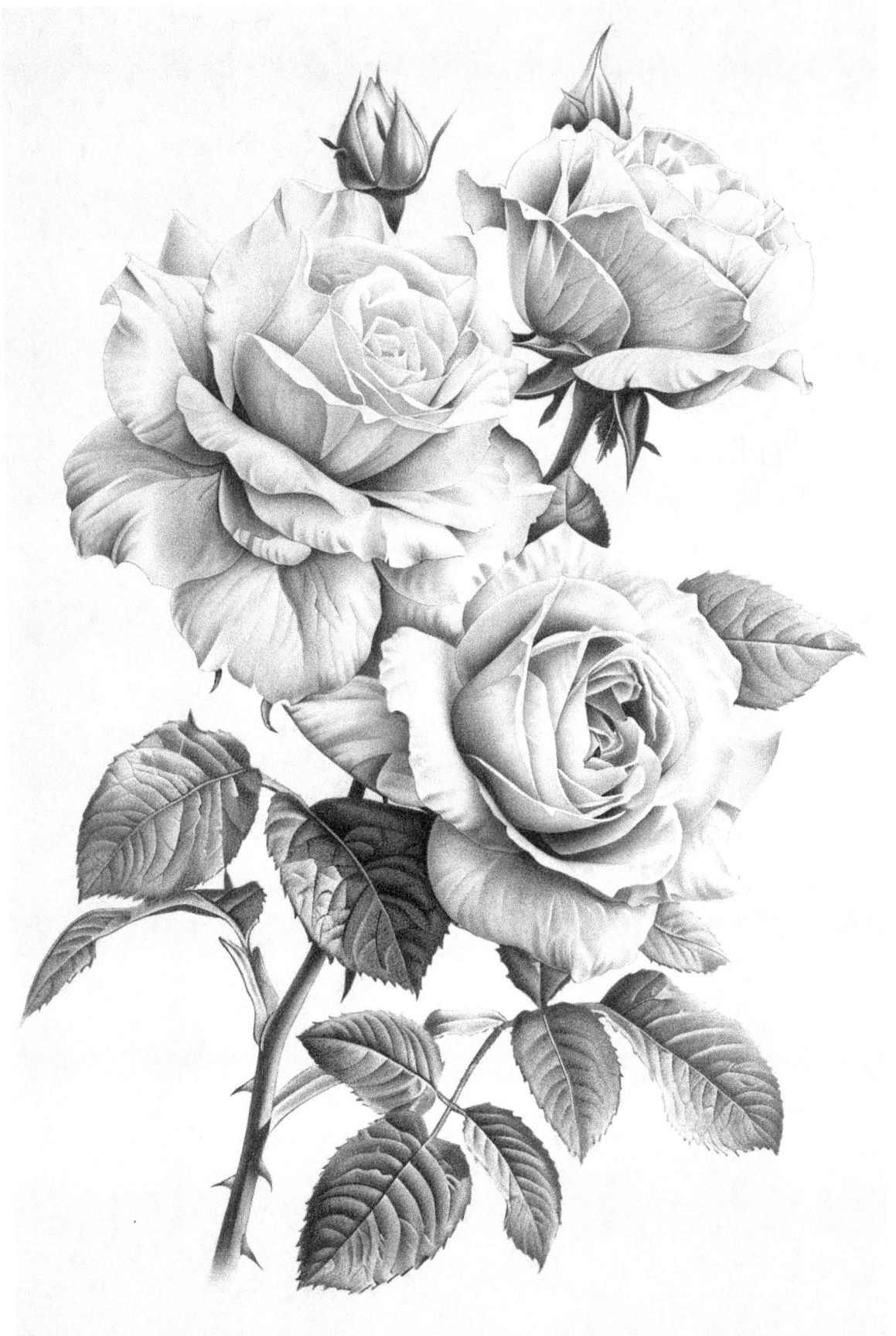

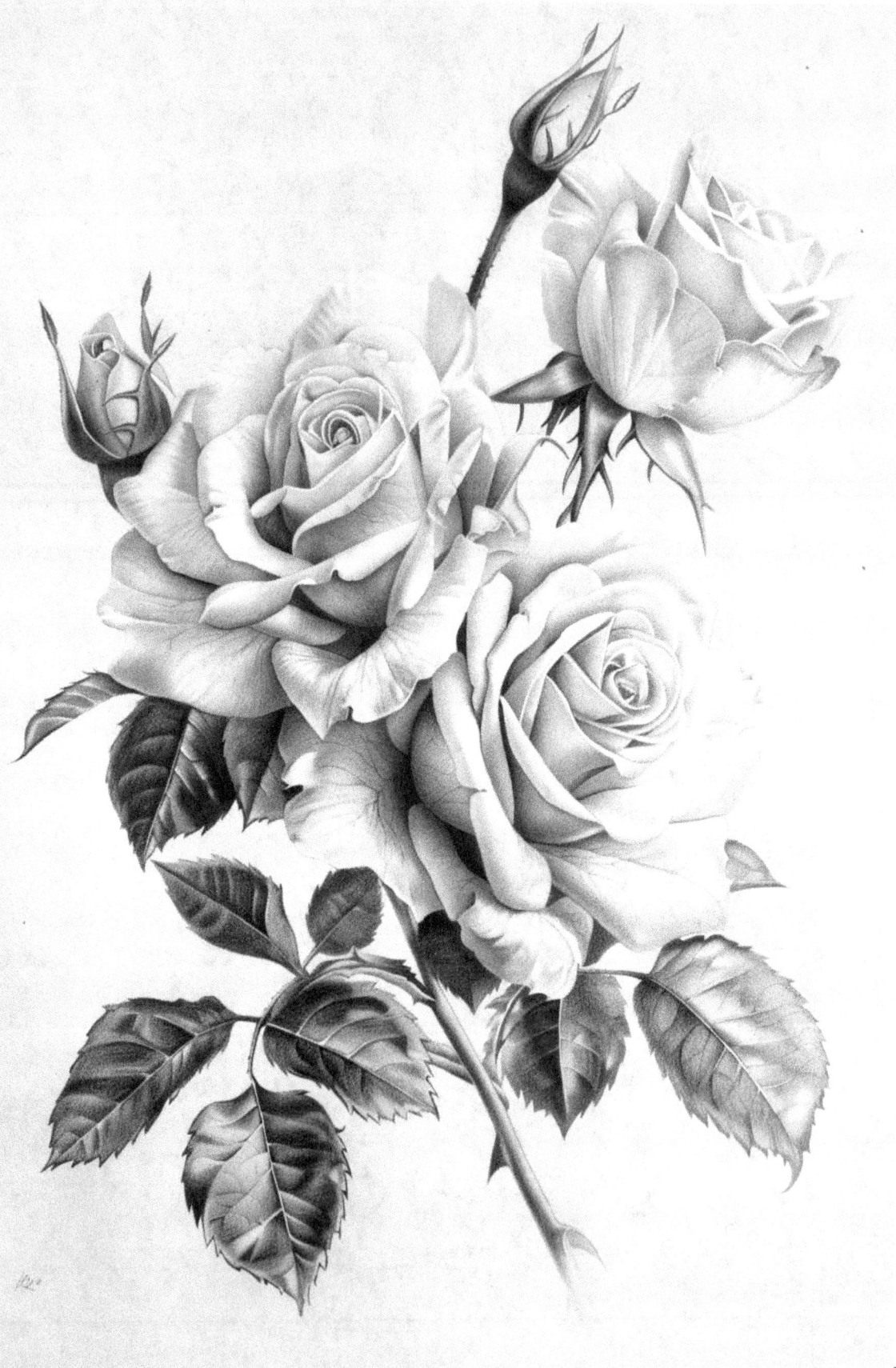

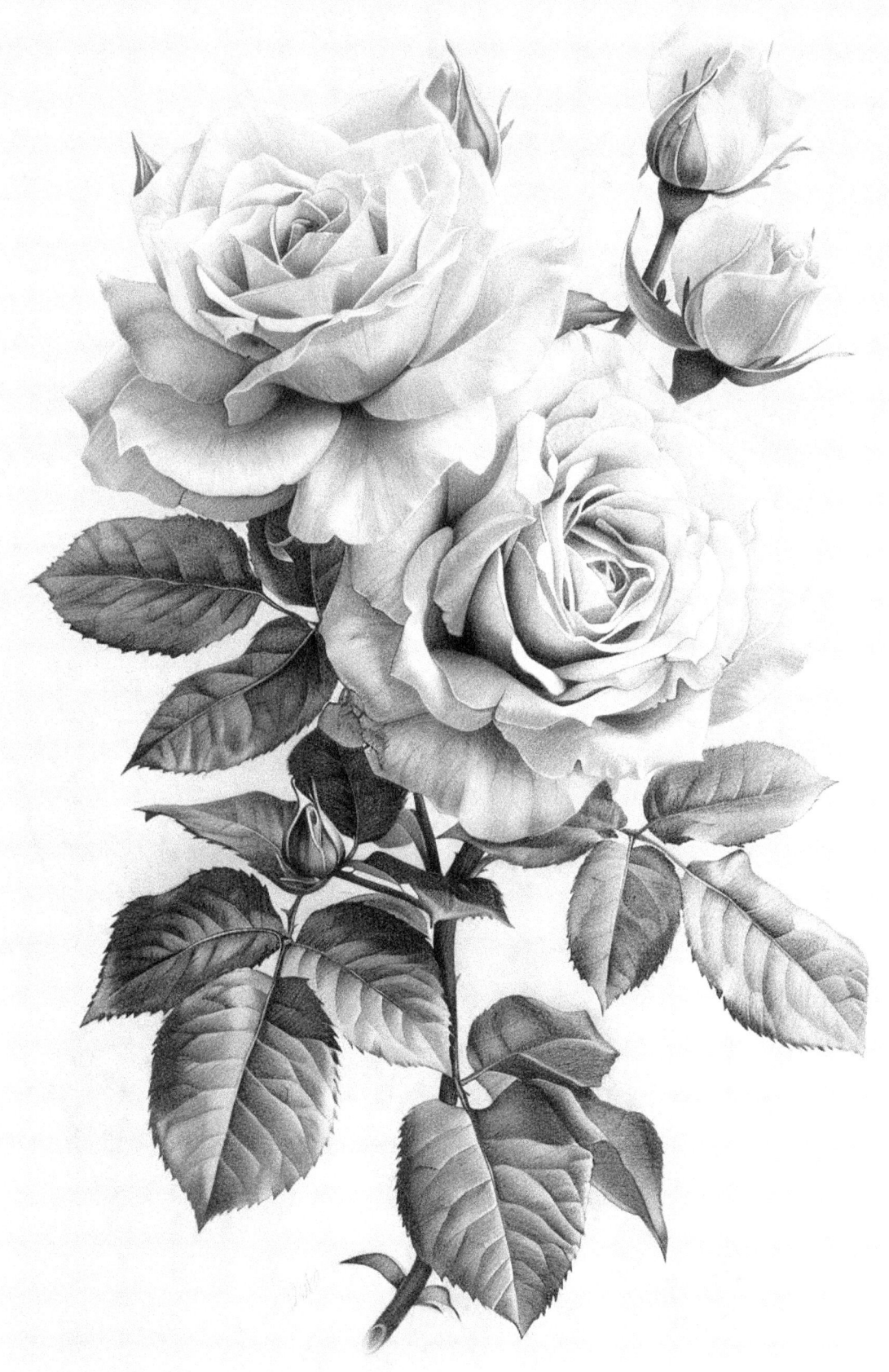

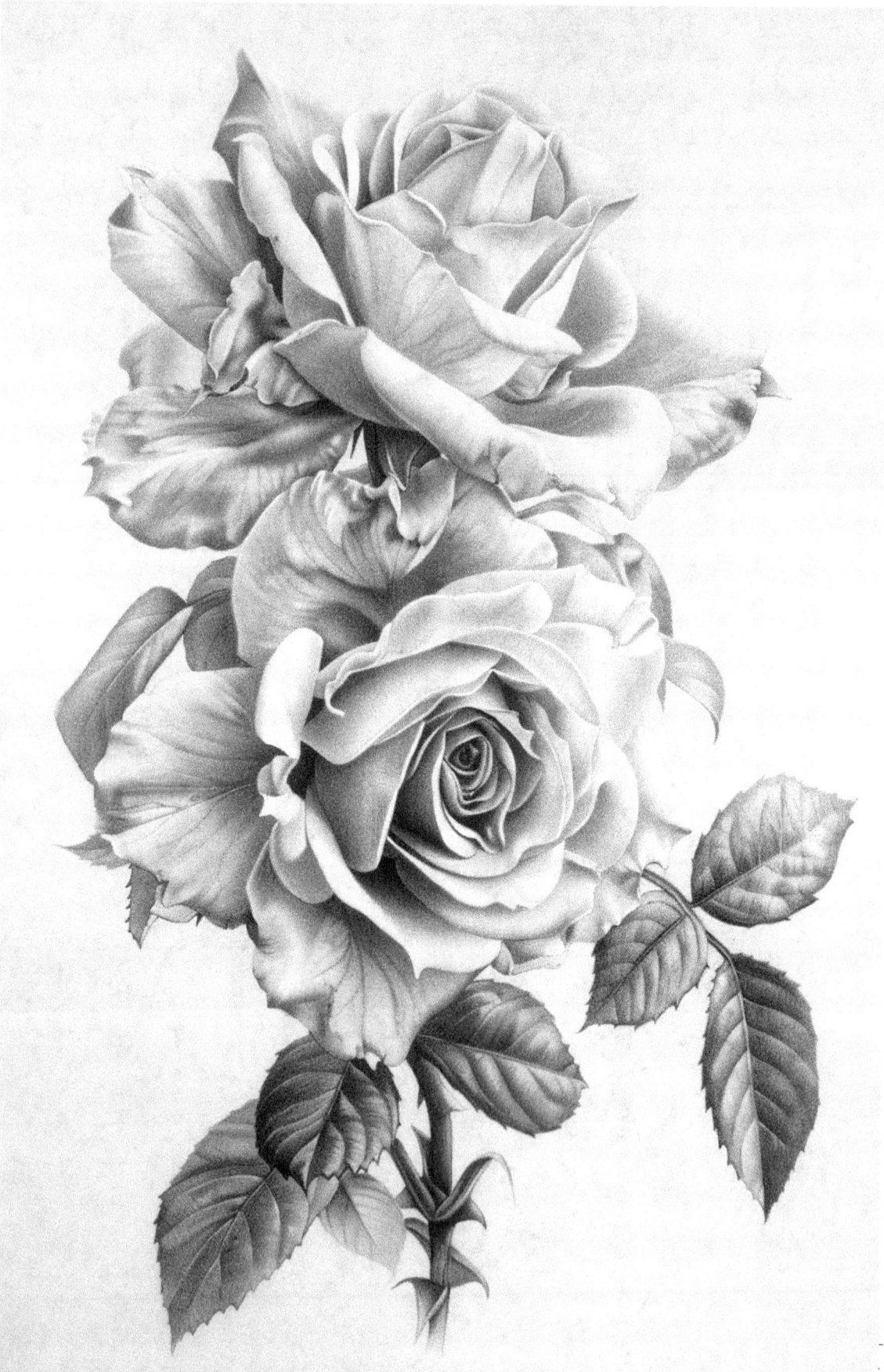

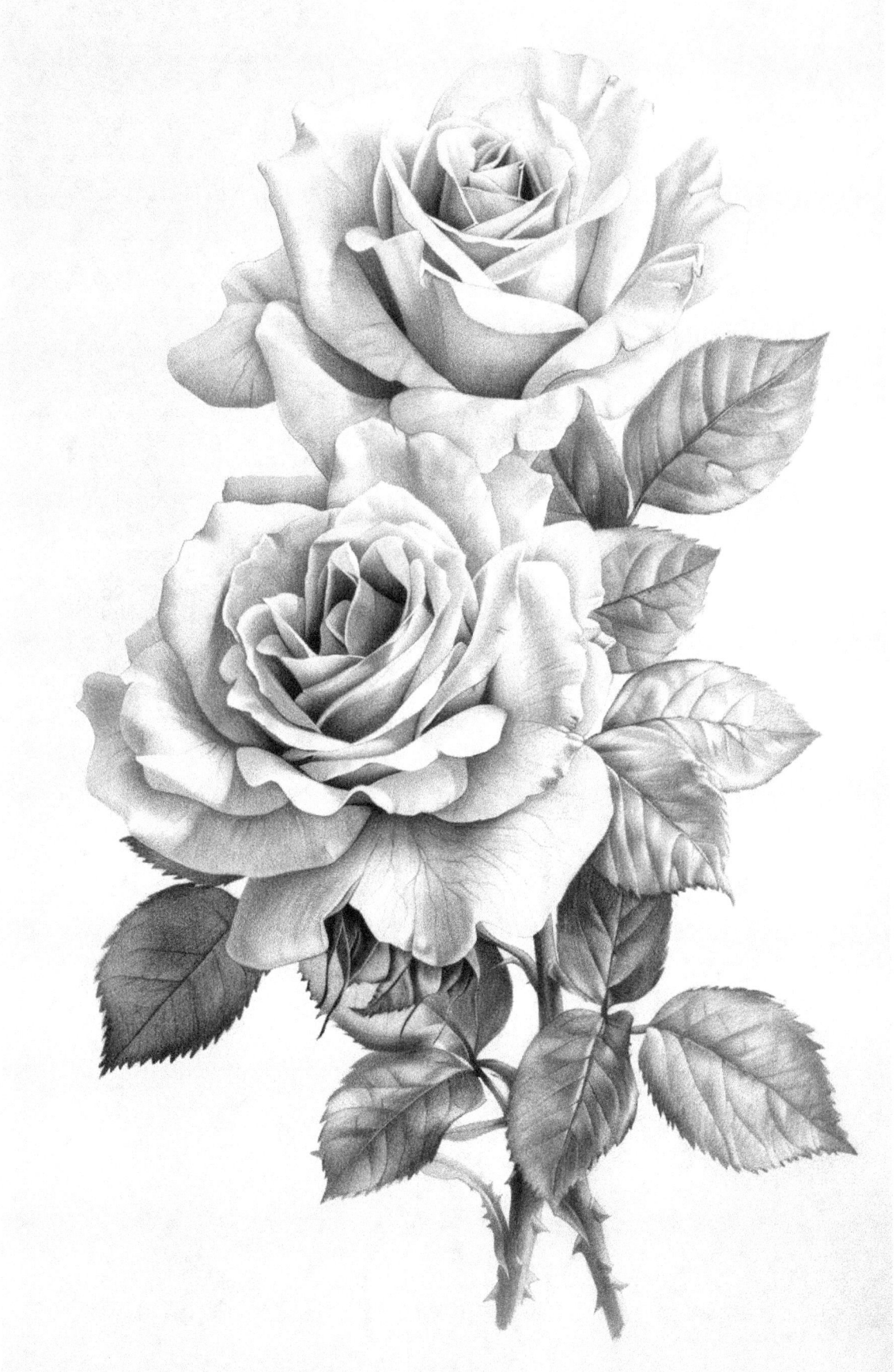

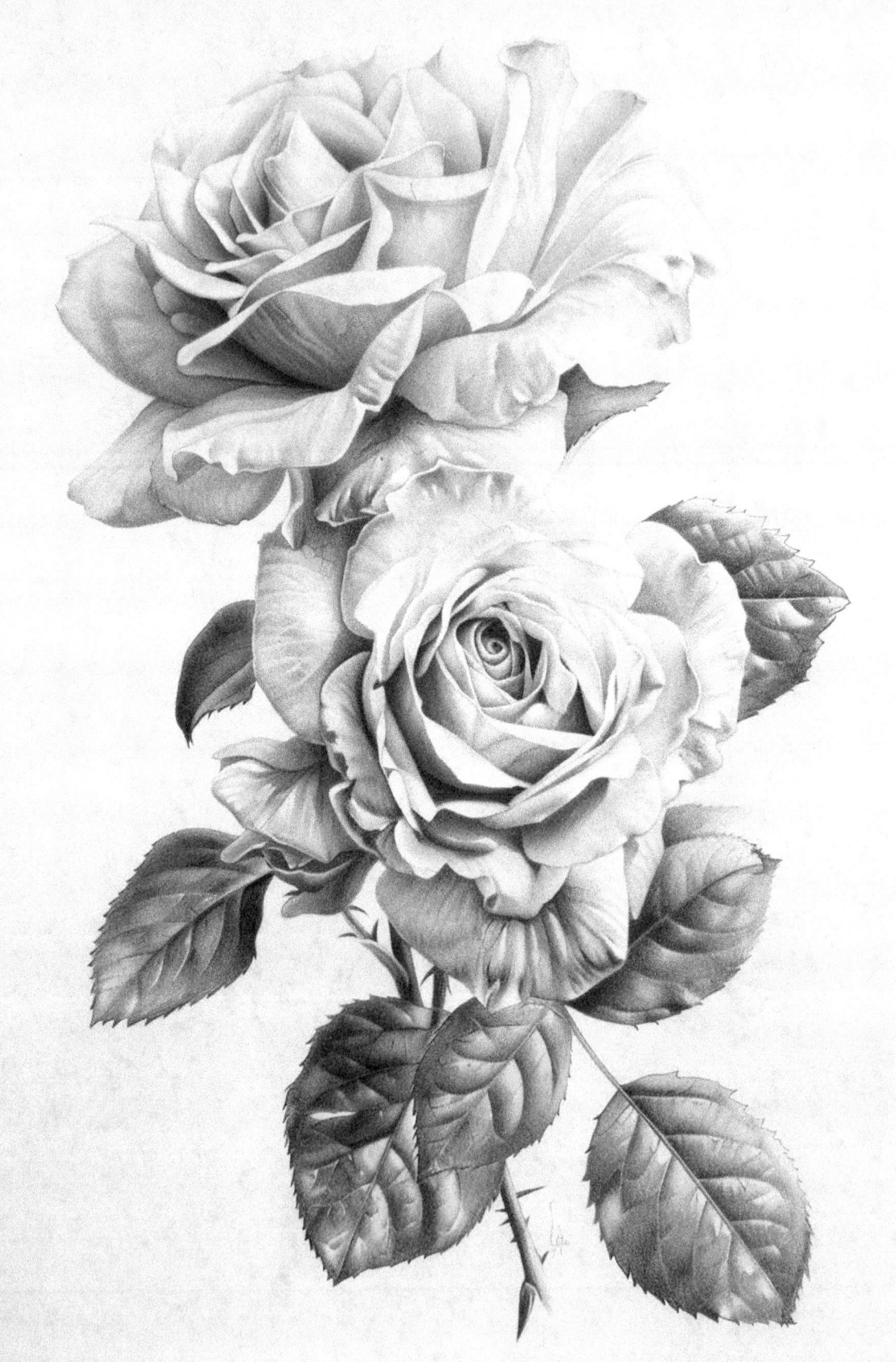

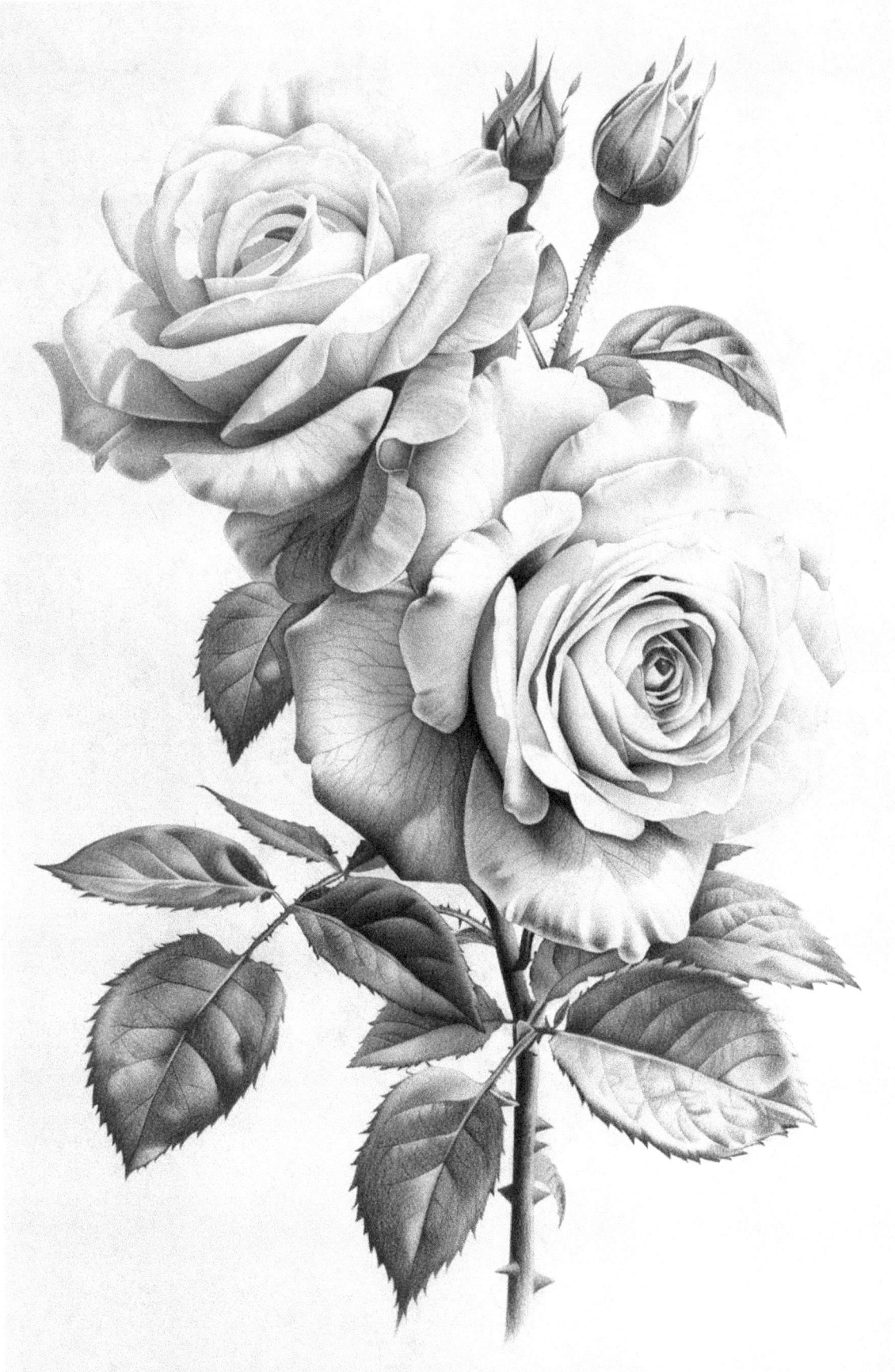

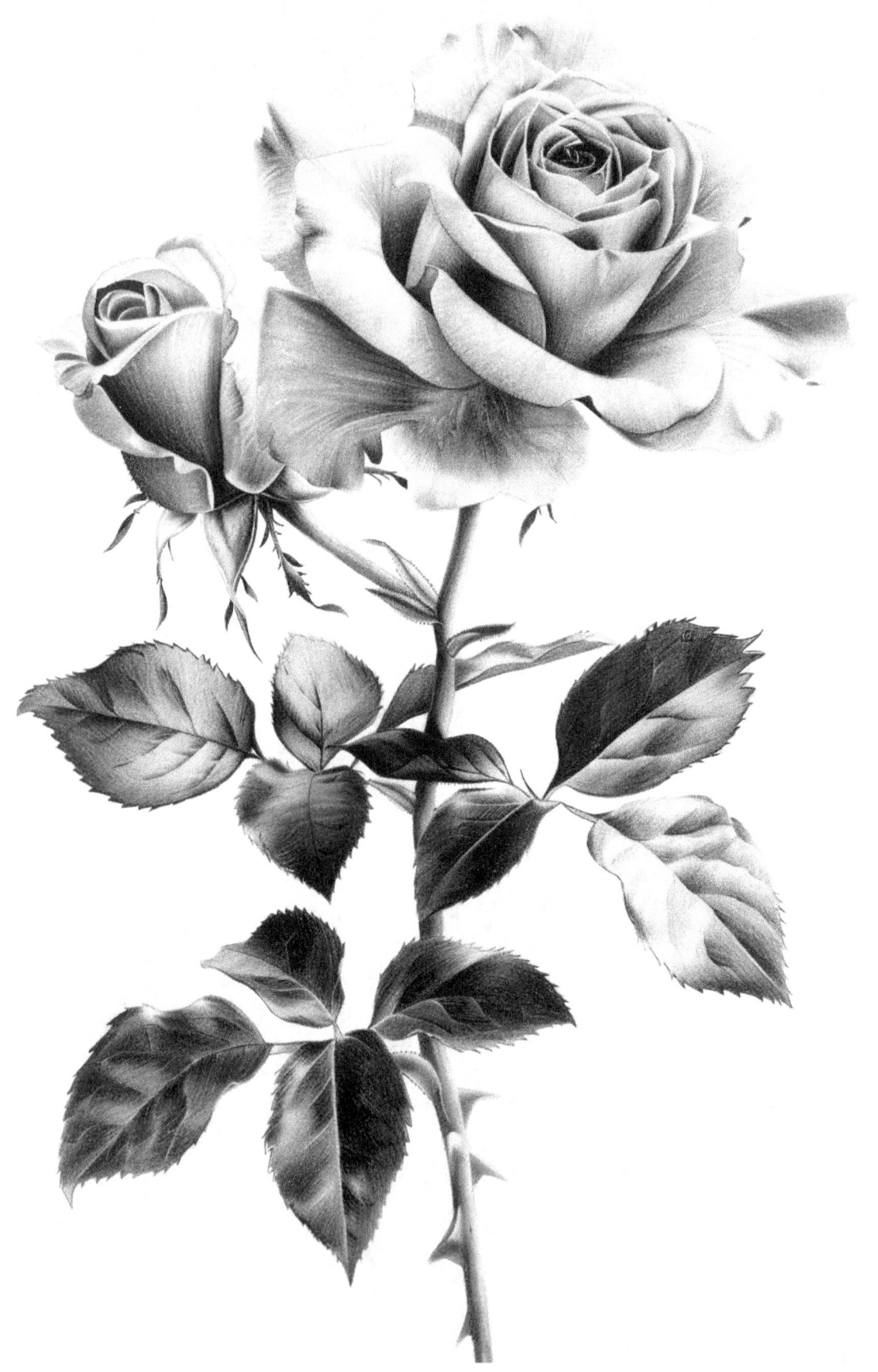

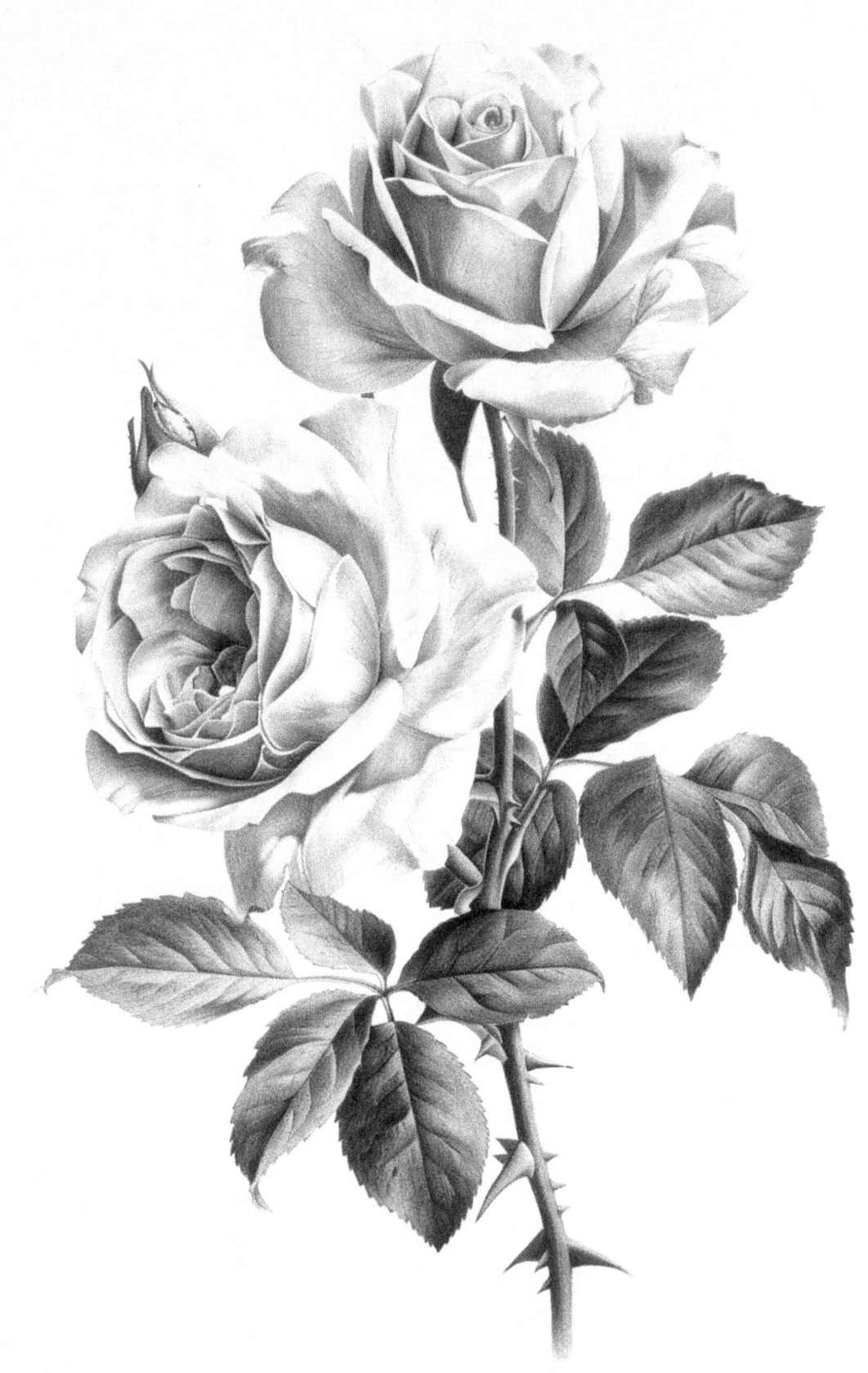

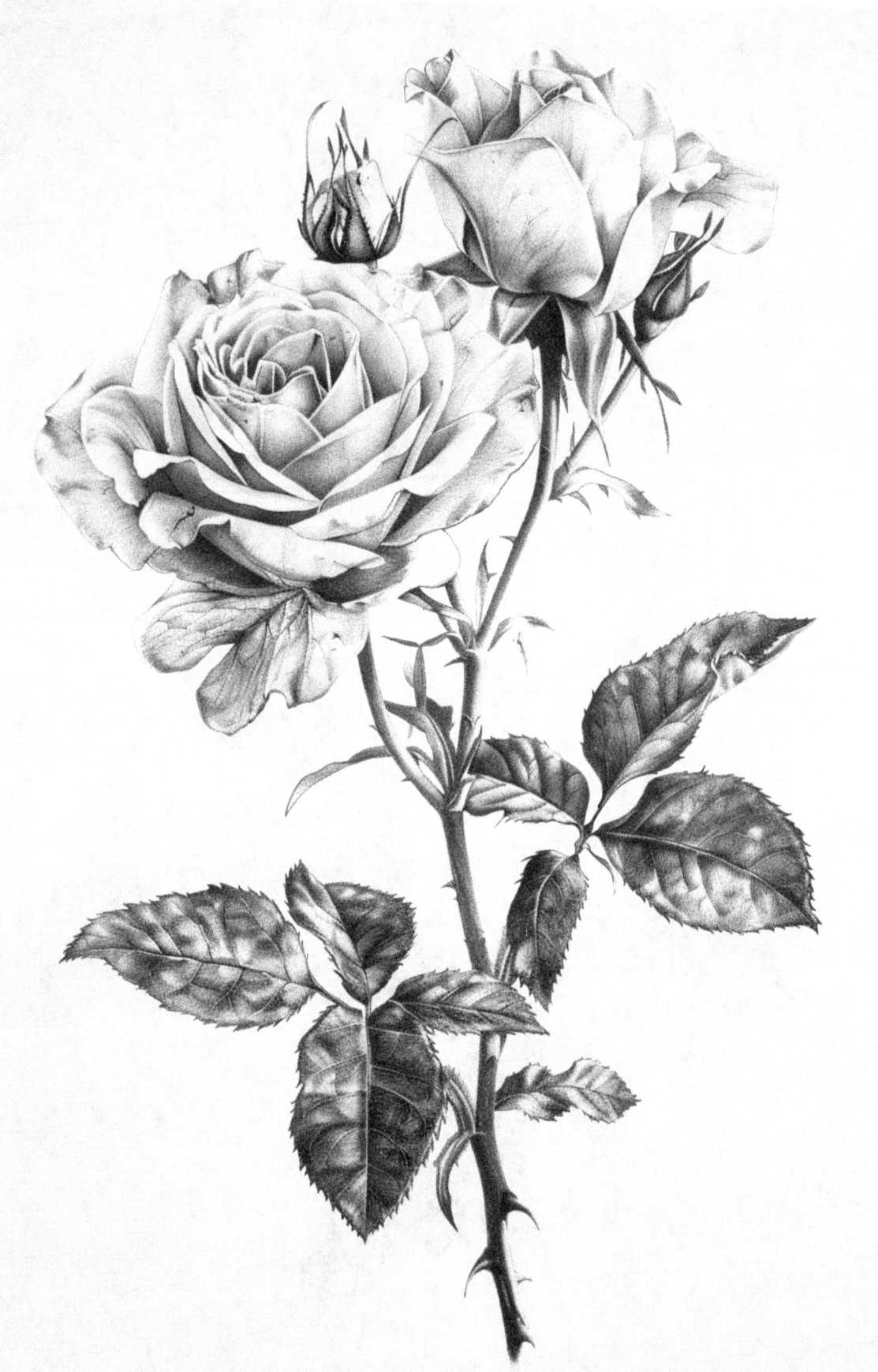

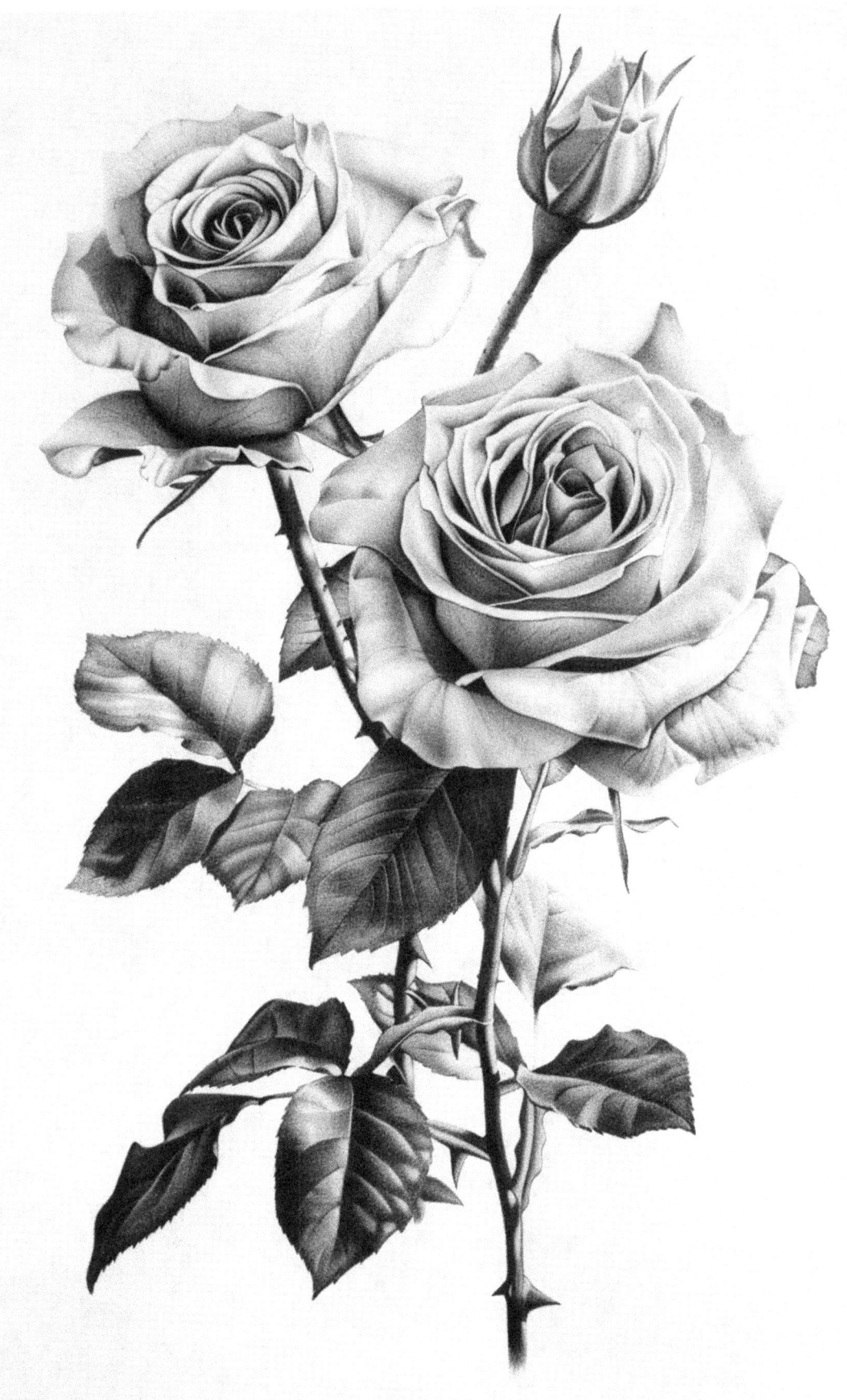

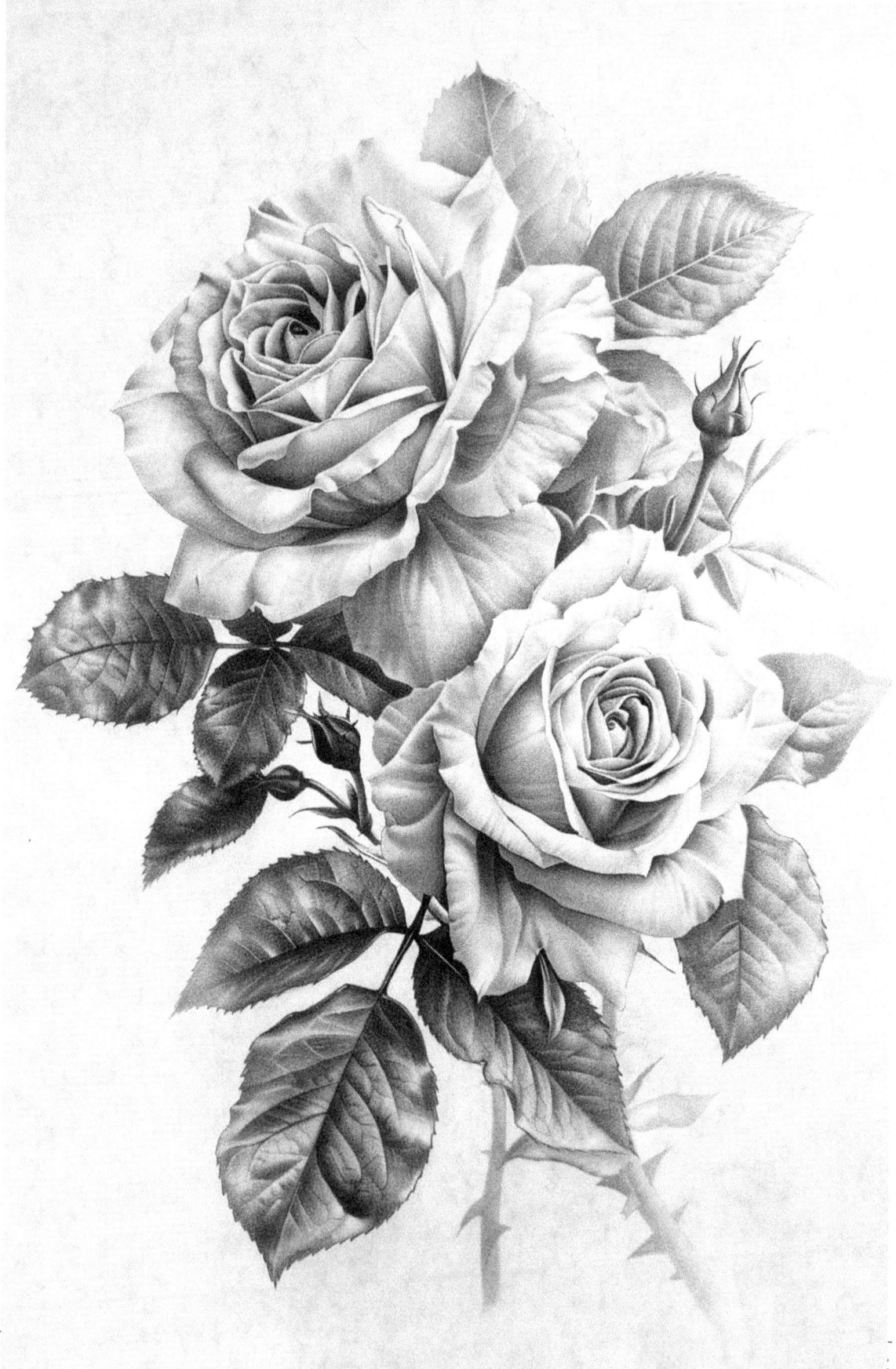

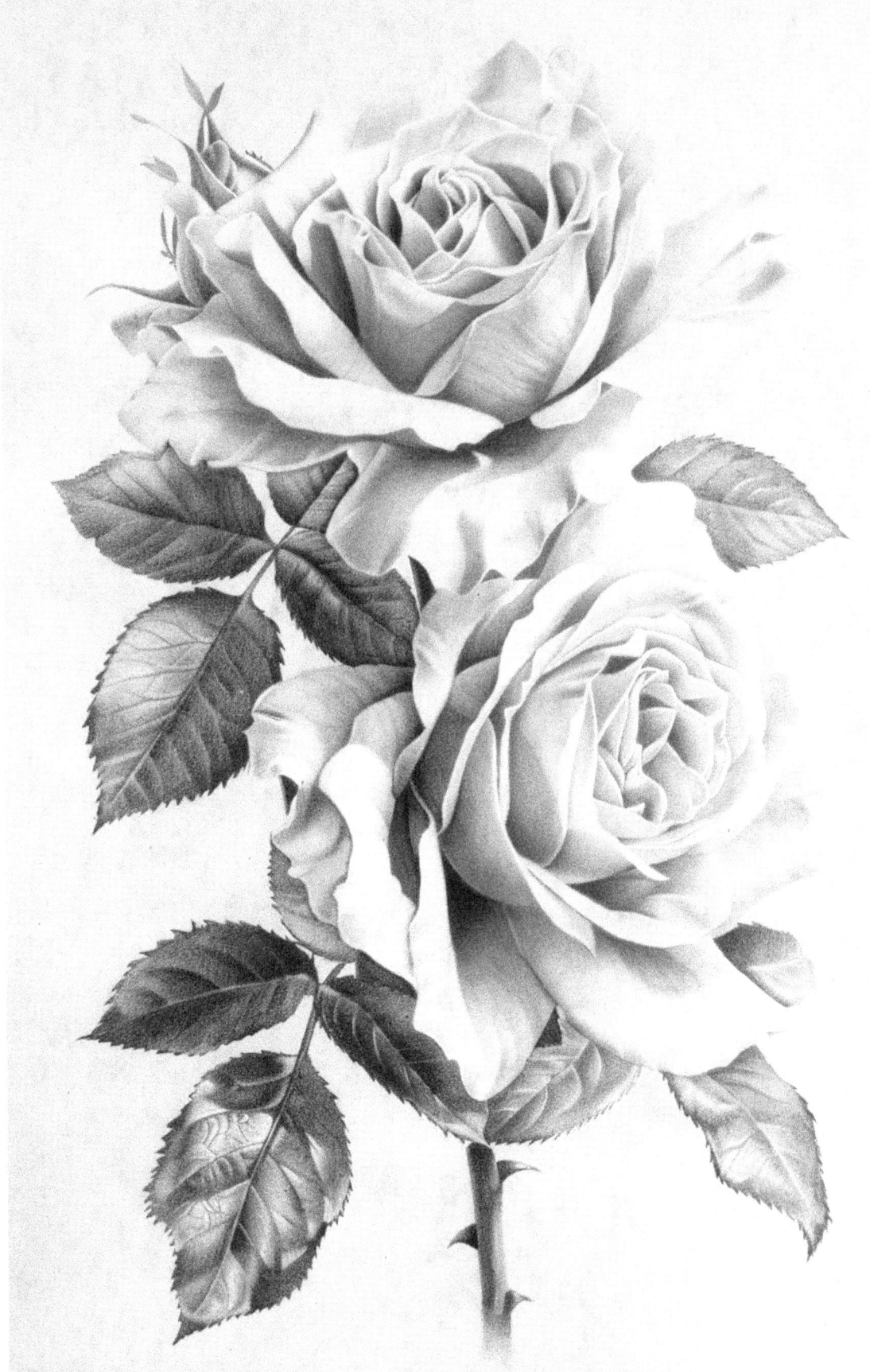

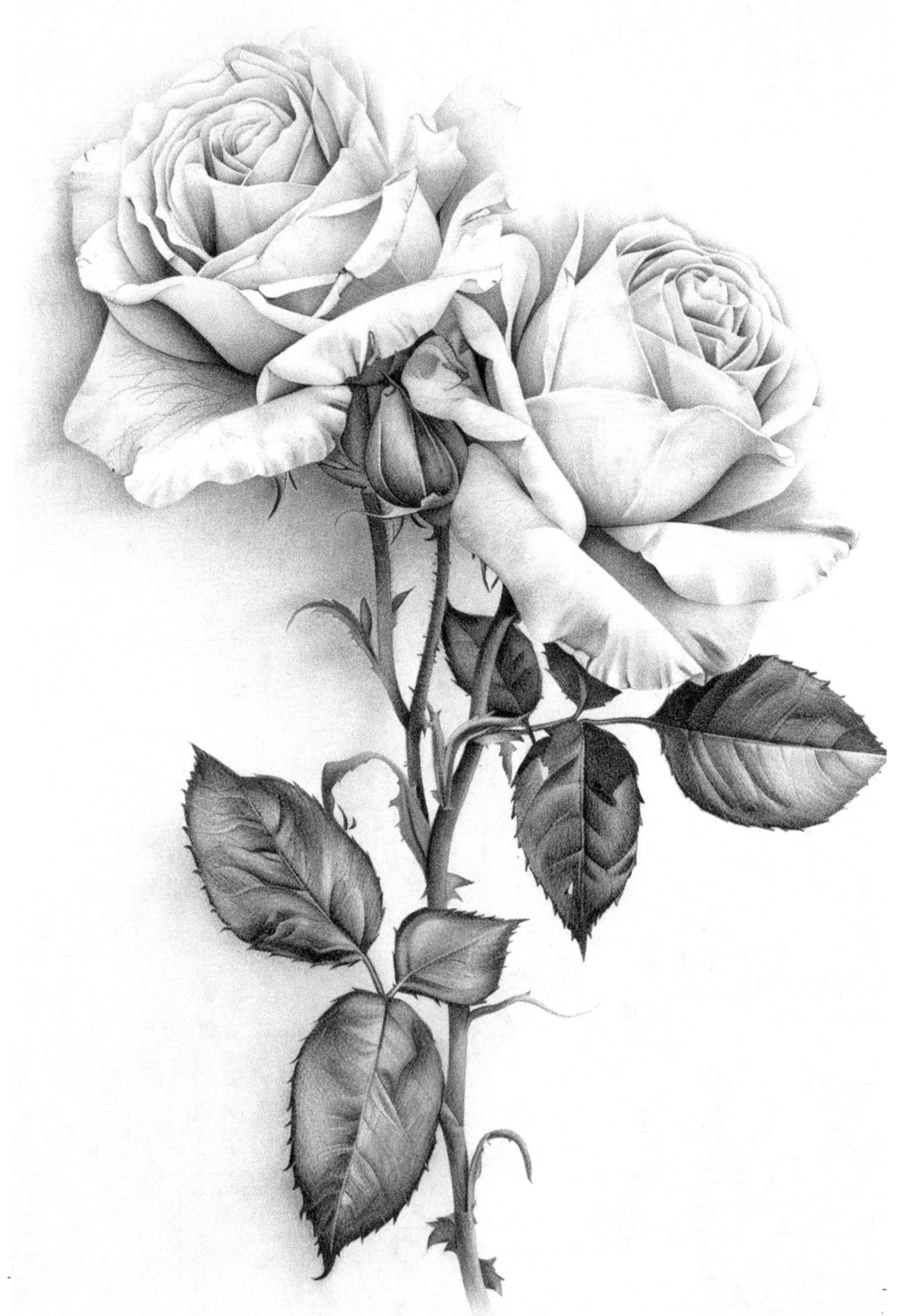

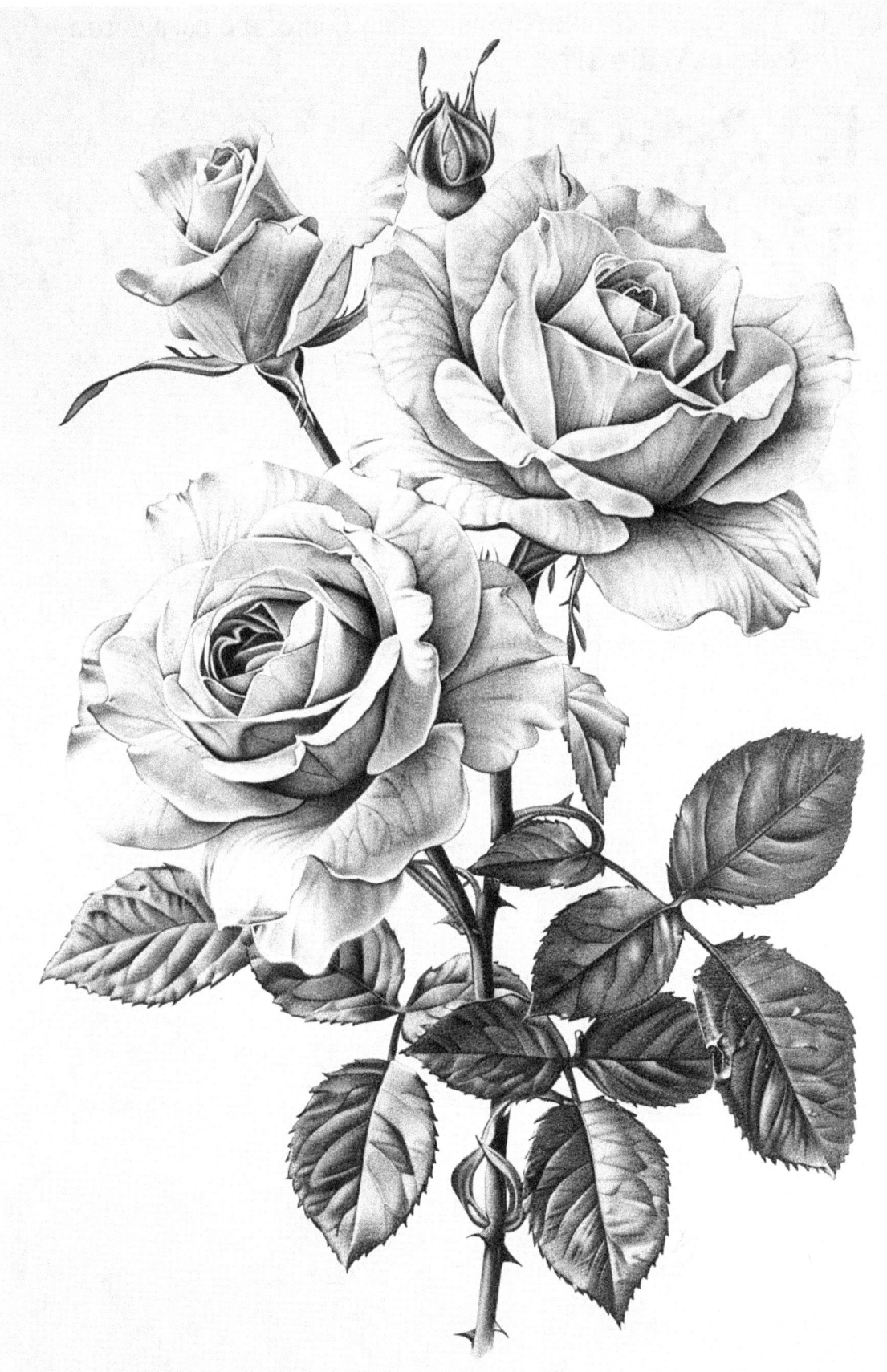

Scan the QR code below to download and enter the password :
**RosesBlackWhite3!**

 If the download does not work or for any question, contact us at Facebook
https://www.facebook.com/DivineTattooDesign

# HOW TO PREVENT PAGES FROM COLOR BLEEDING

If you like to use this book as a coloring book here are the ihjnstruction to totally prevent color bleeding ftom pages even when using acrylic inks to paint the pages.

Now how about making those pages resistant to color bleed of the markers ? There are 2 easy ways to do it.
We have to apply <u>LIGHT coat</u> of transparent gesso. Any transparent gesso from art supplies will do

### APPLICATION.

With a sponge brush or another light flat brush ( take care to have a correct bigger size – optimal is 1-2 inch brush for that) , dip the brush to the gesso , dry it , remember we want only a little and apply to the page evently,one pass will do.
It needs very little and thin layer, let it dry for 10-15min. you may apply a second pass if necessary please experiment on a blank paper to see if it needs. Usually it does not. Make sure the book is open while it dries so the pages do not stick together..

We need a little we do not want to go aggressive to the paper and wet it too much or deform it.

You will find a video about it in my YouTube Channel. Scan the below code to go to my video or the channel and search for "
Learn how to stop color bleeding of markers and inks from coloring book pages." video demonstration. .

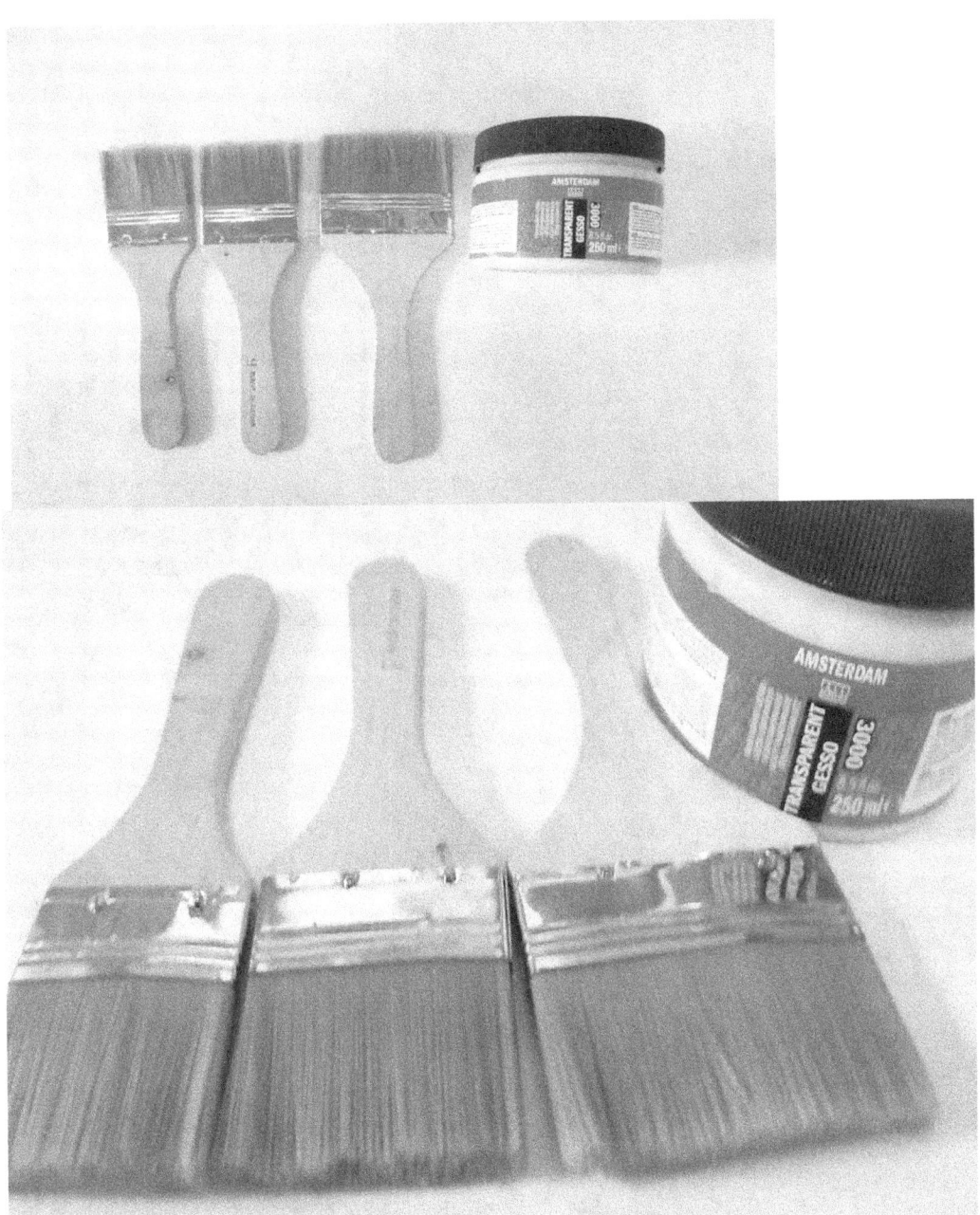

Notice the brushes are flat and thin. The <u>Transparent</u> Gesso is form Talens- Amsterdam series, but other good quality transparent Gesso from art supplies shop, will do.It just has to be transparent

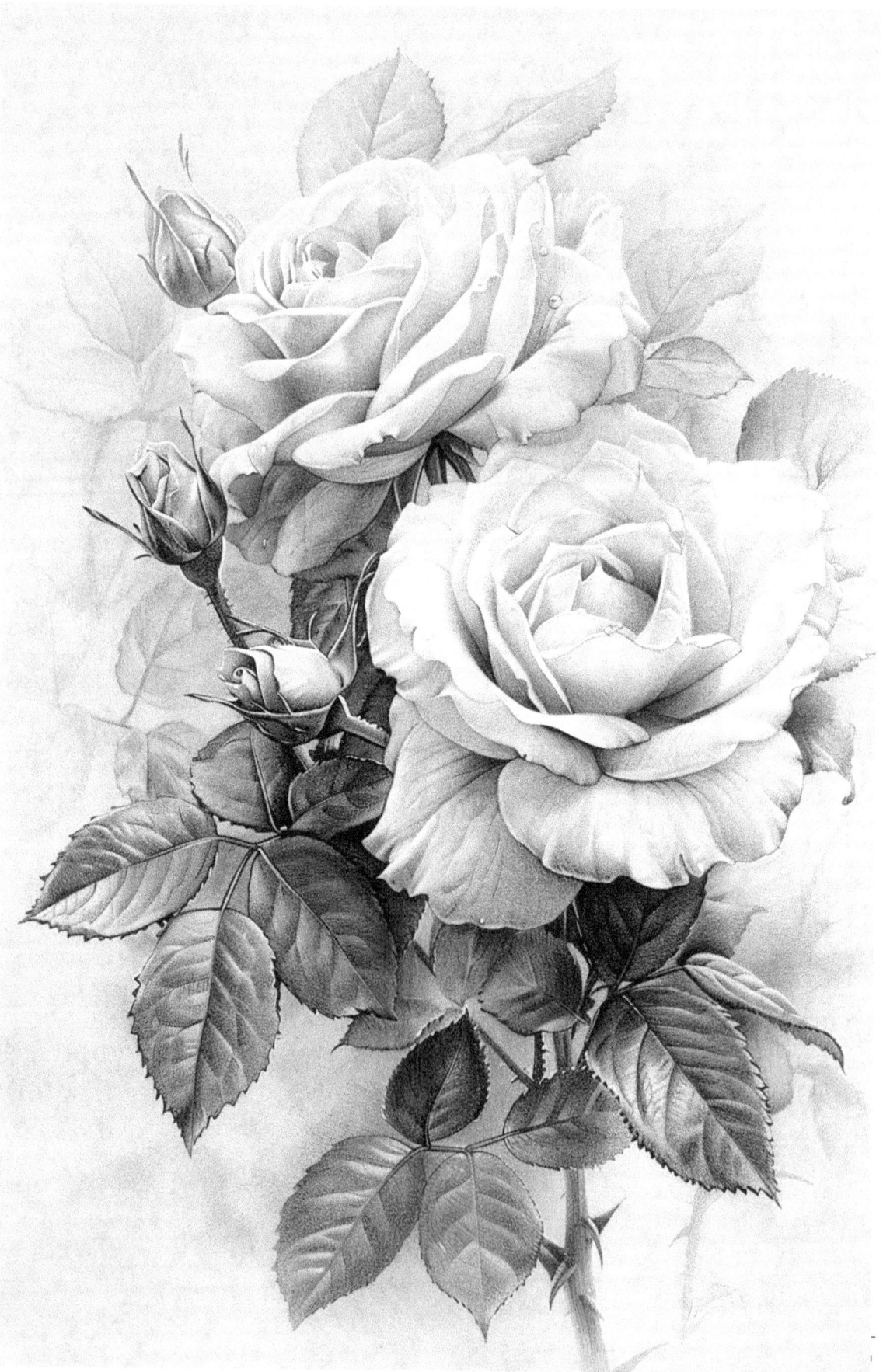

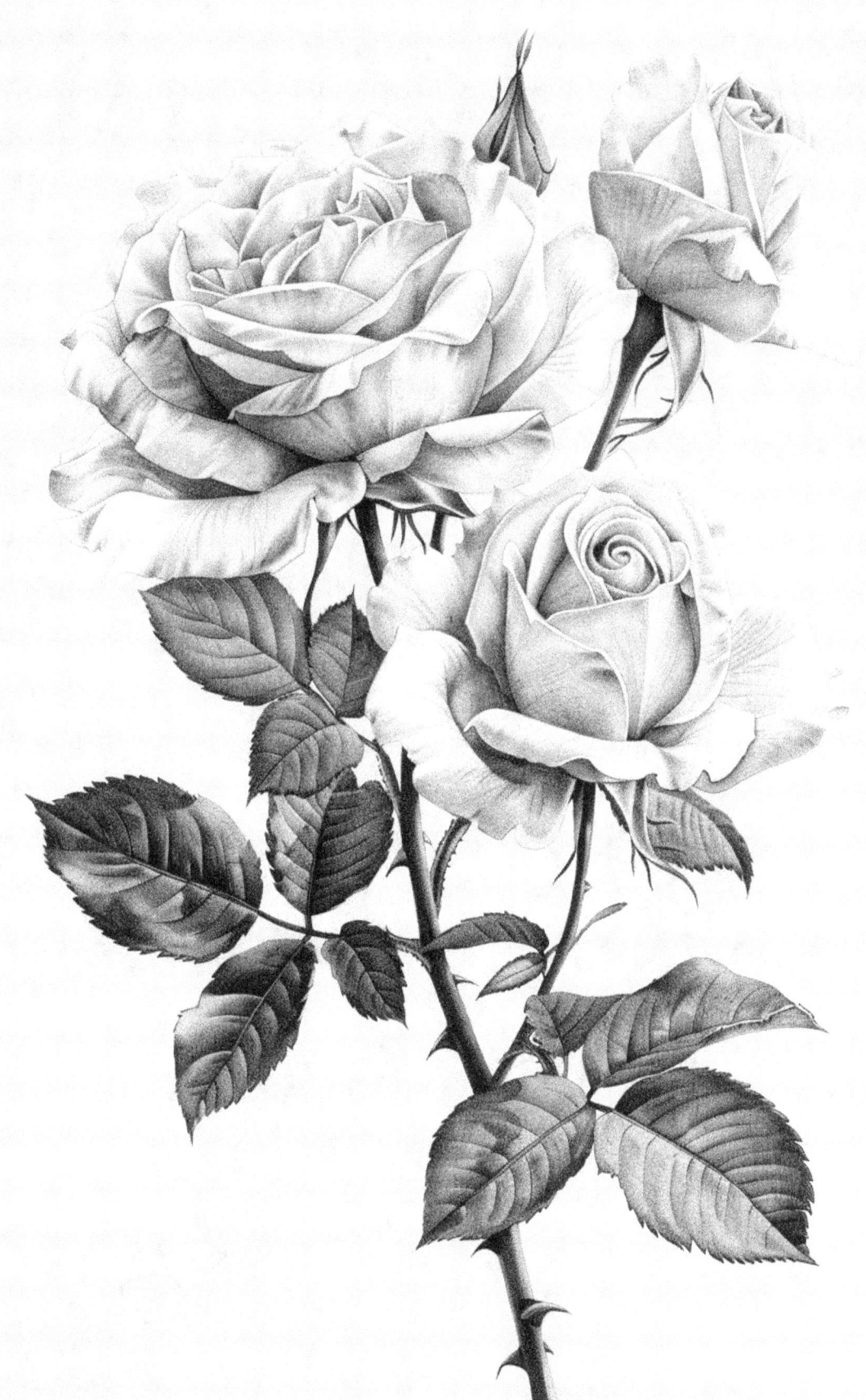

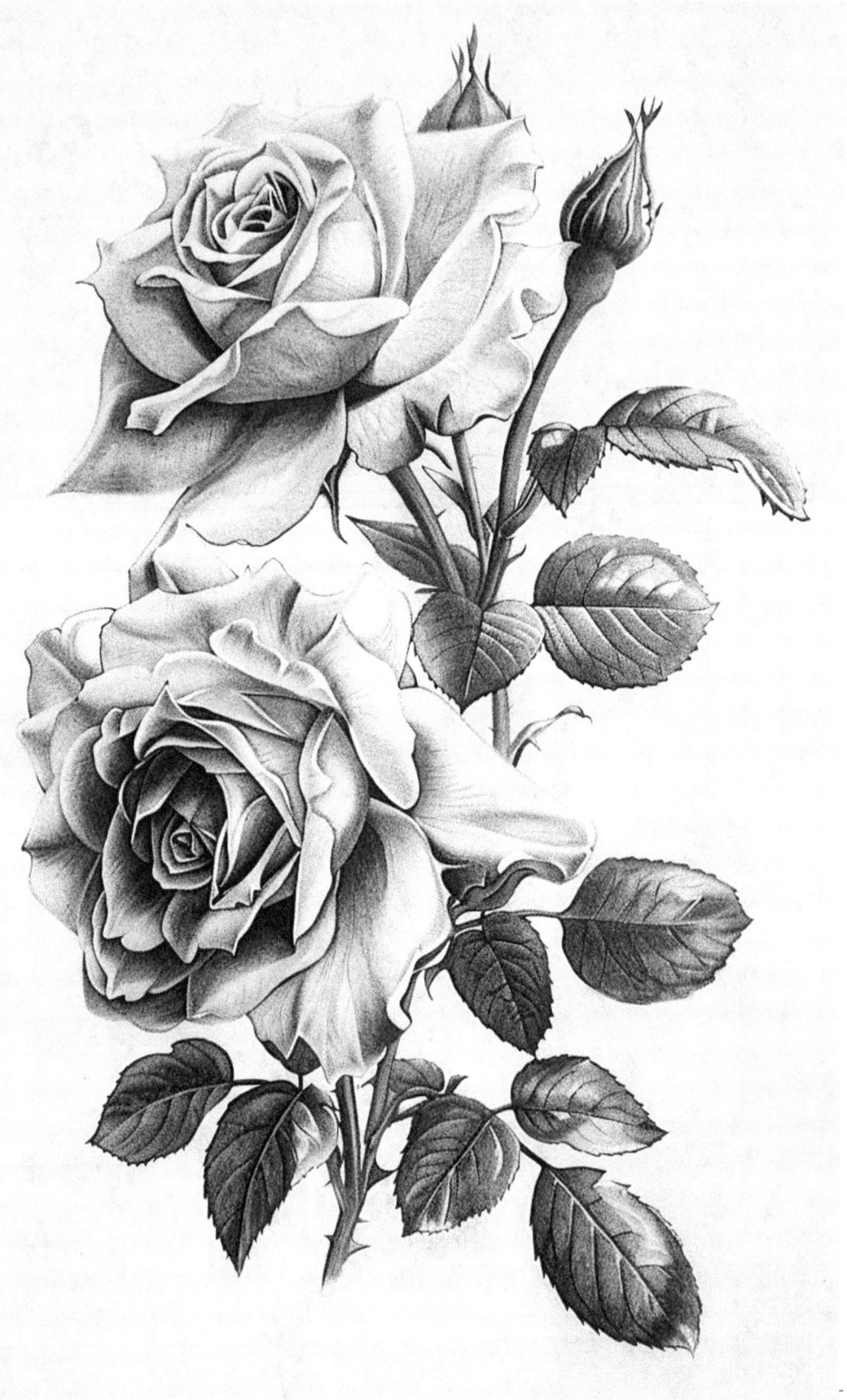

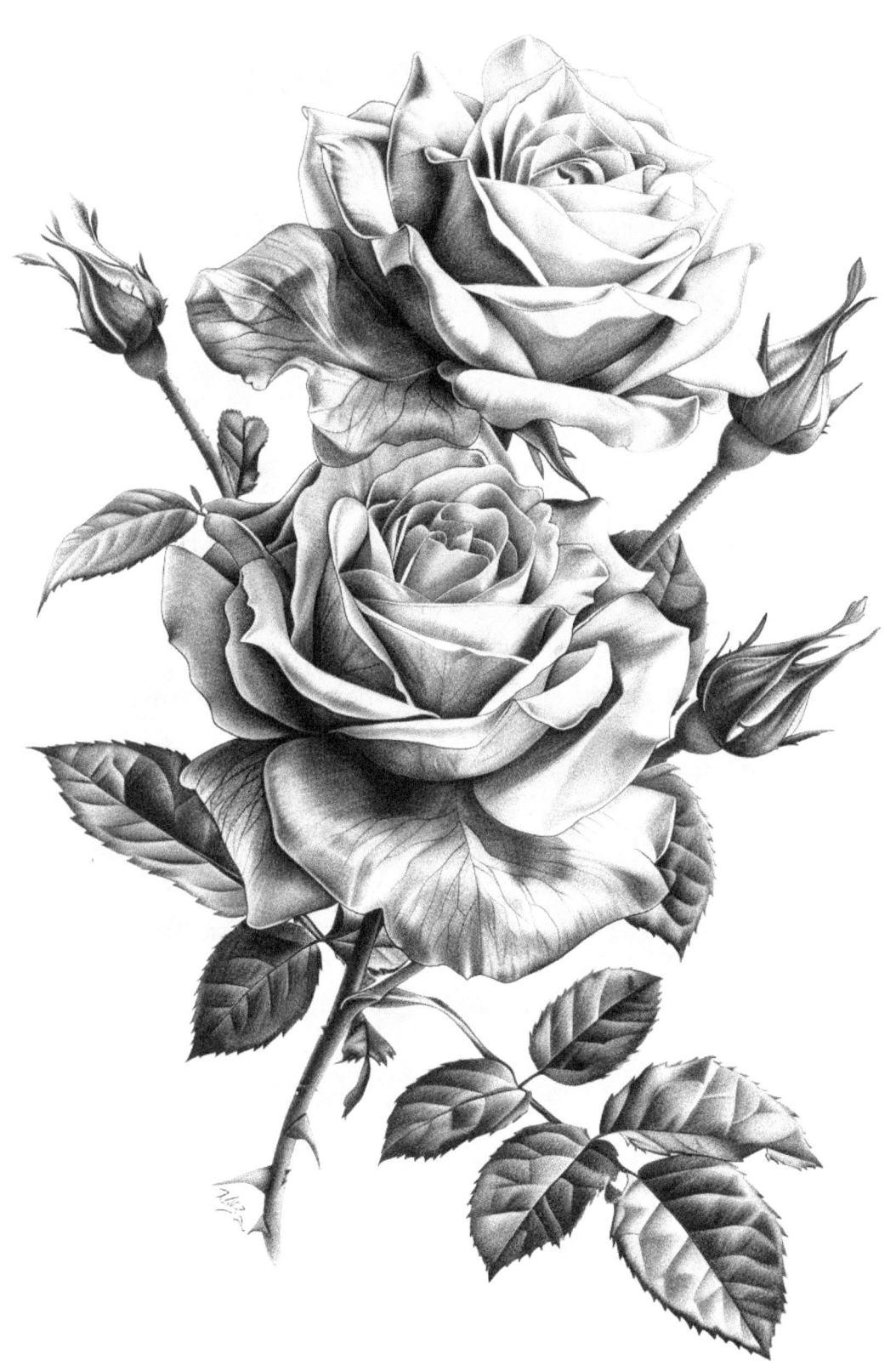

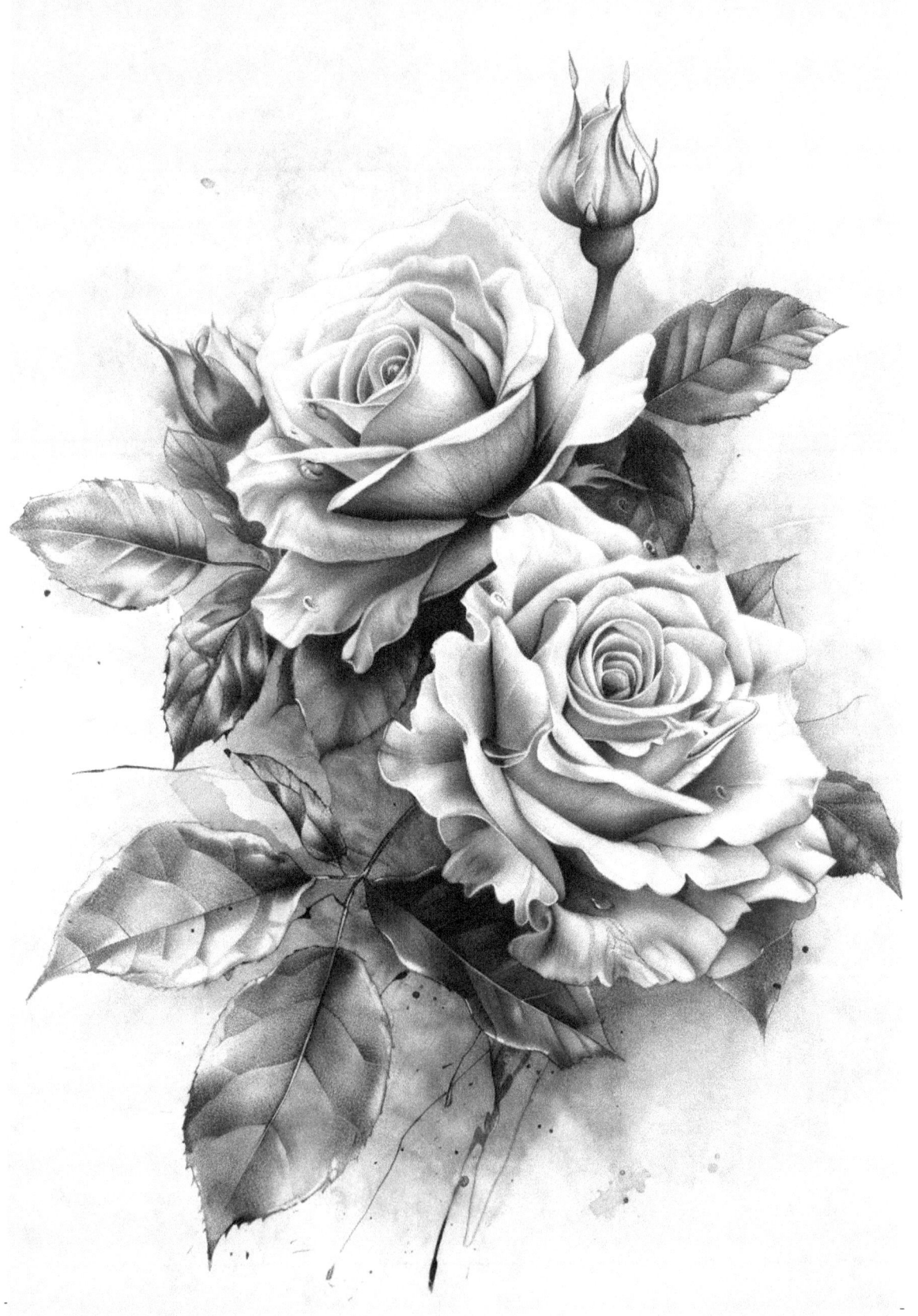

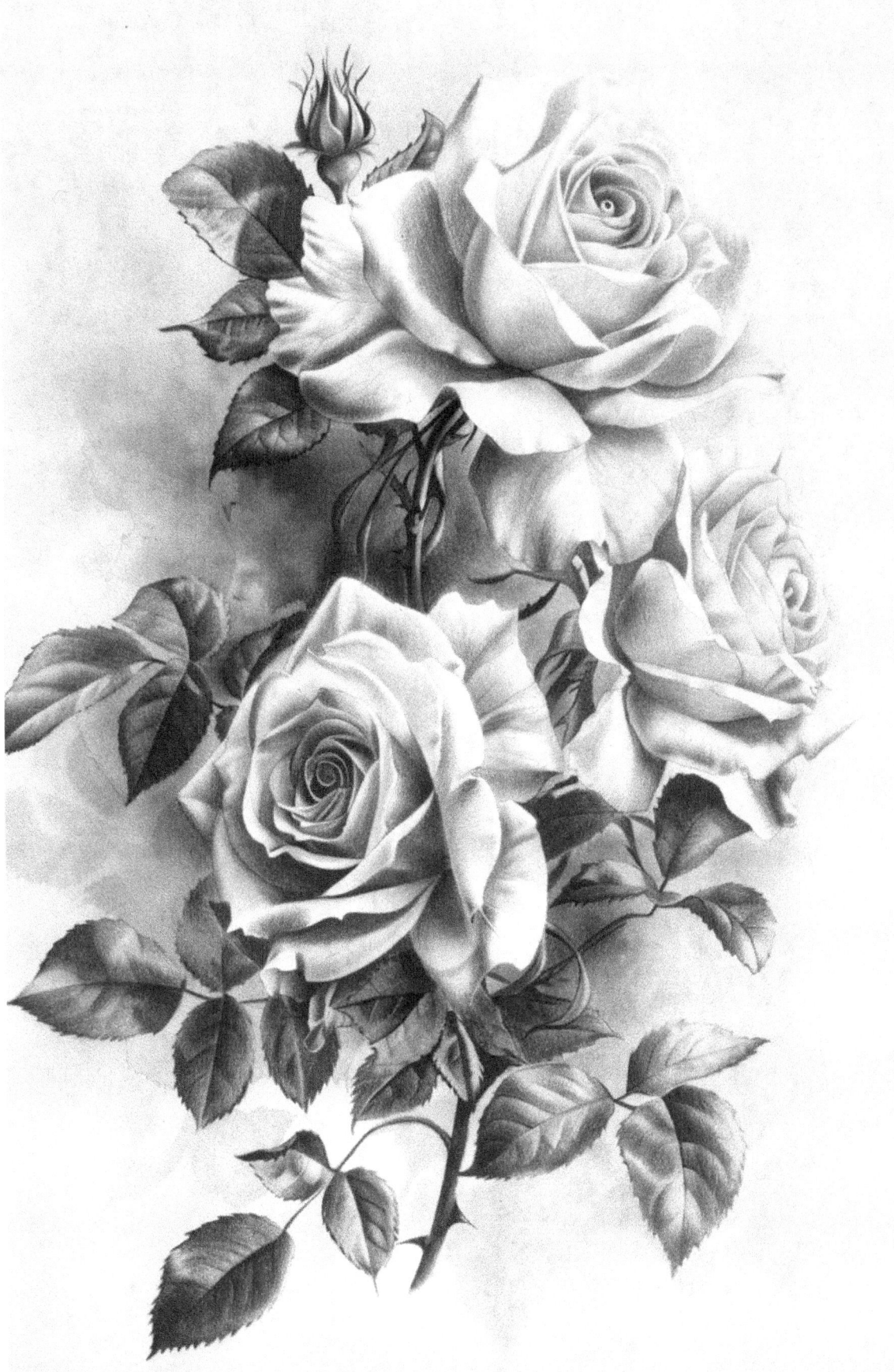

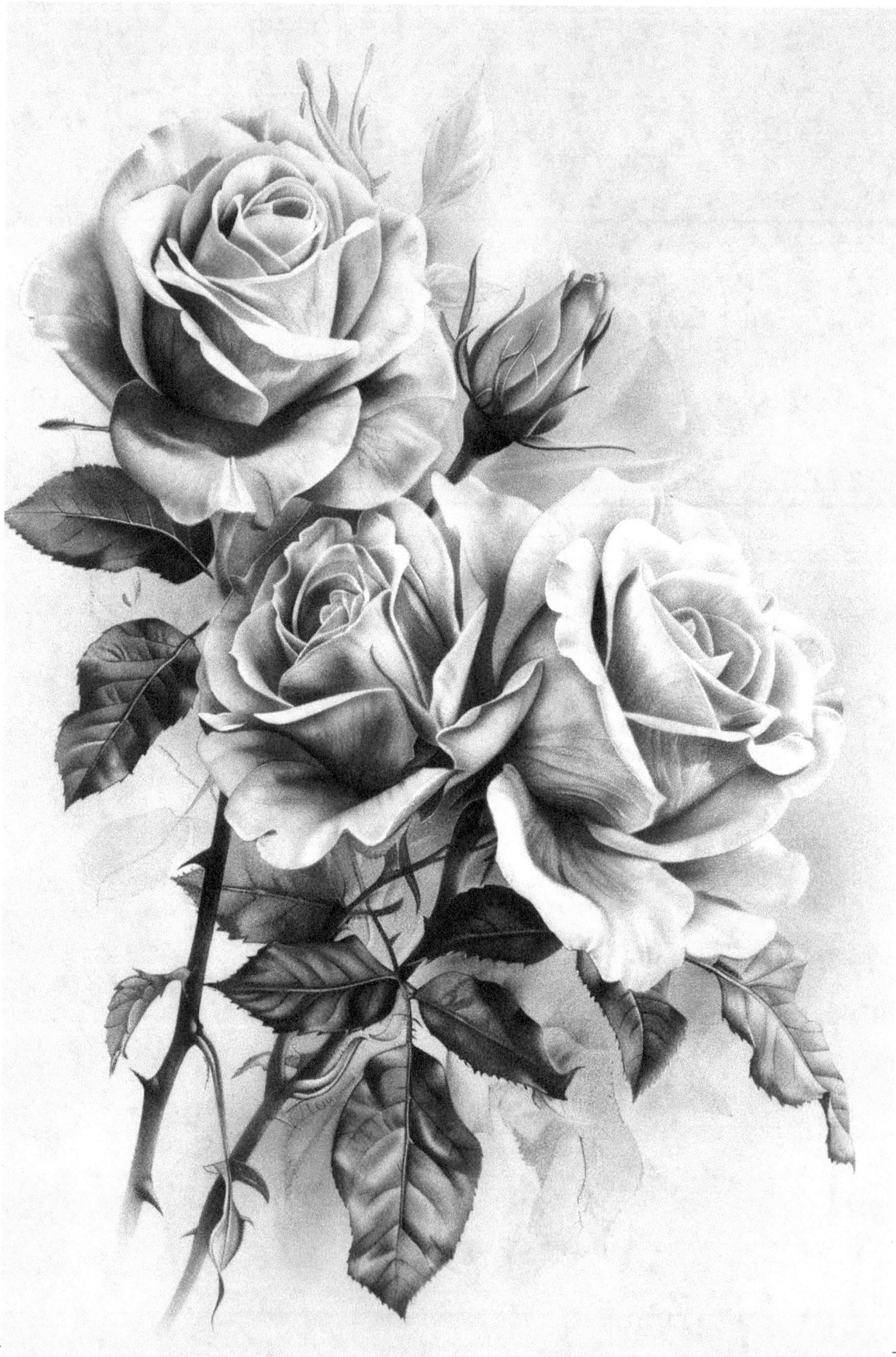

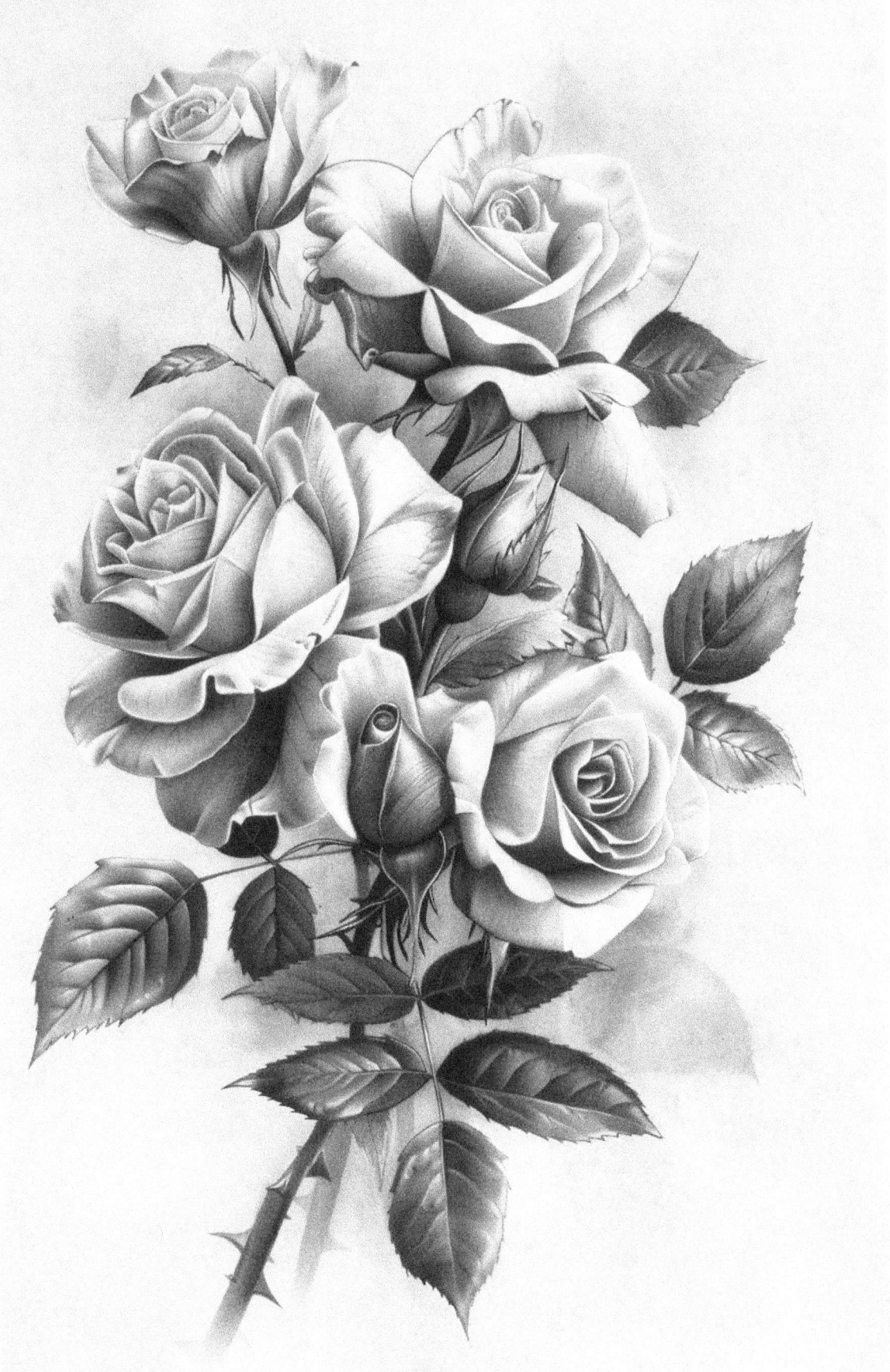

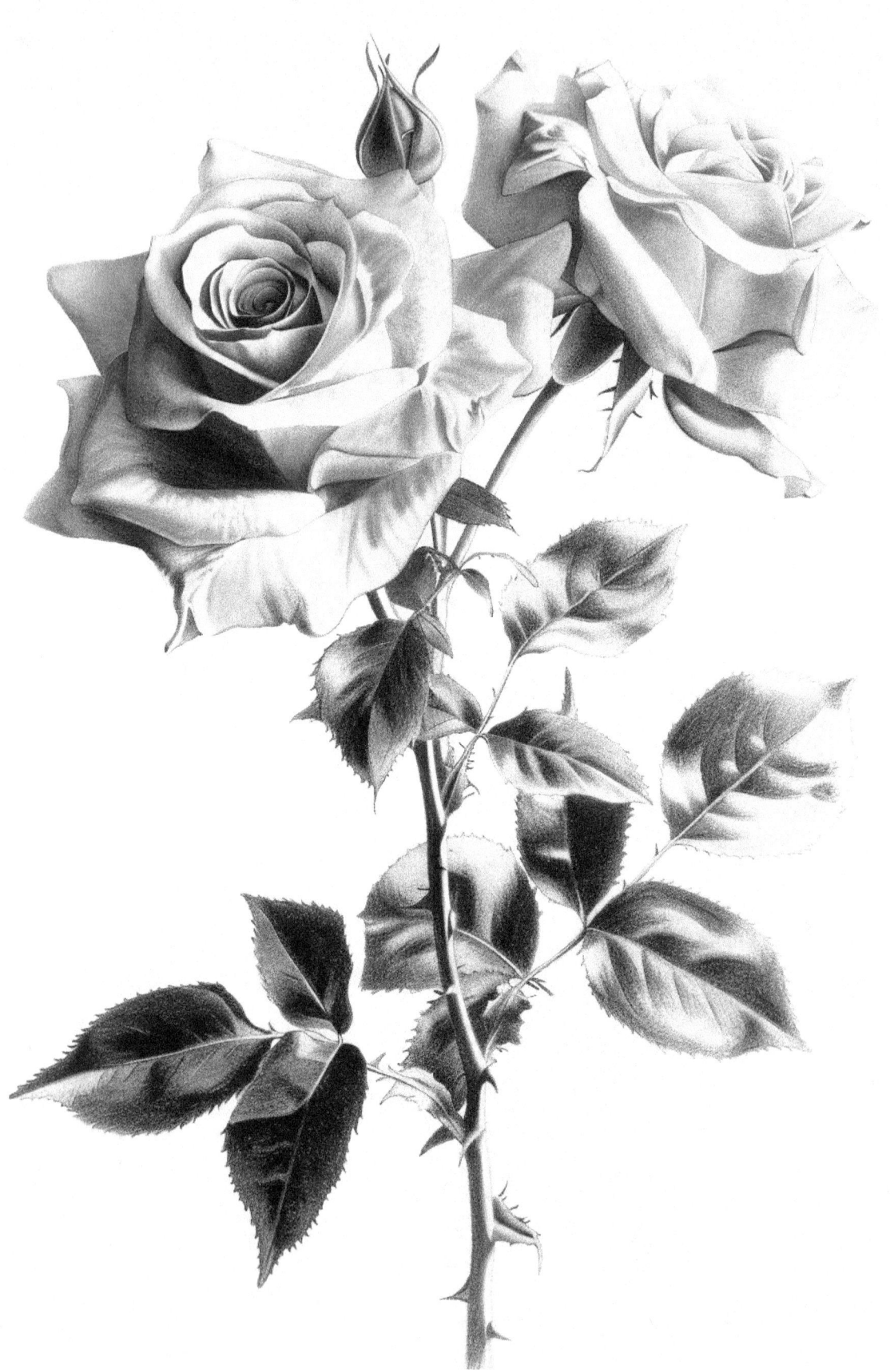

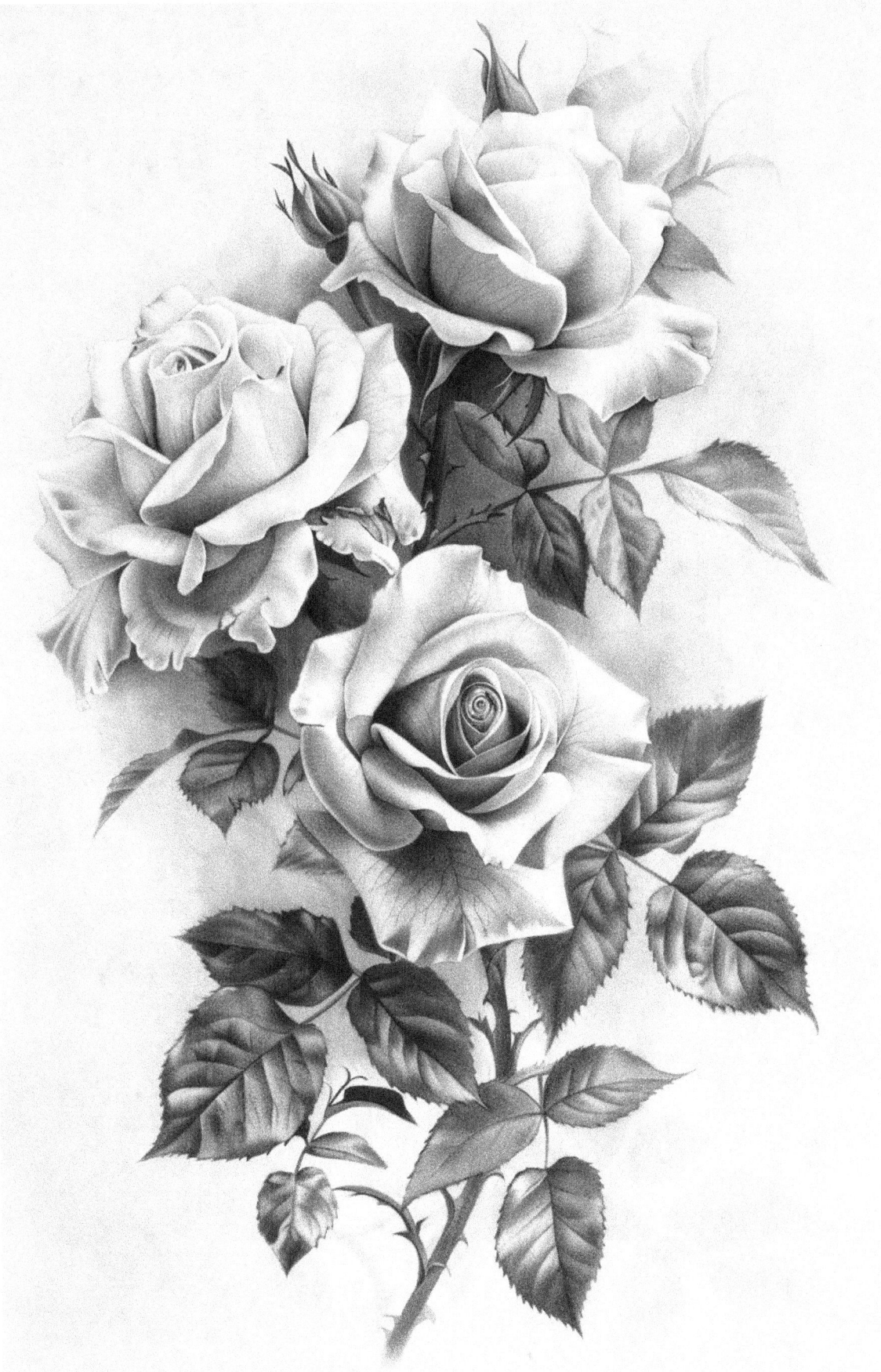

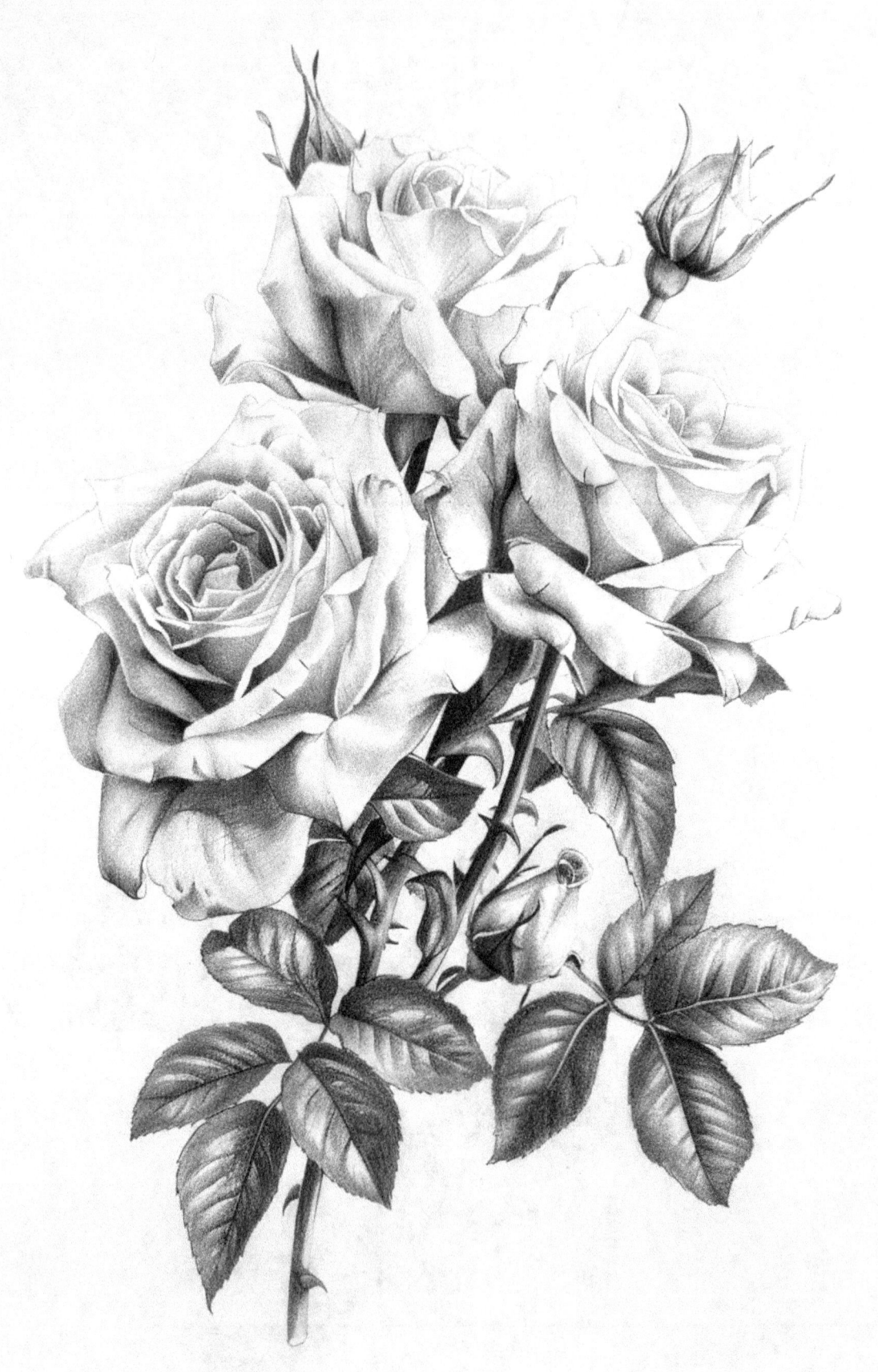

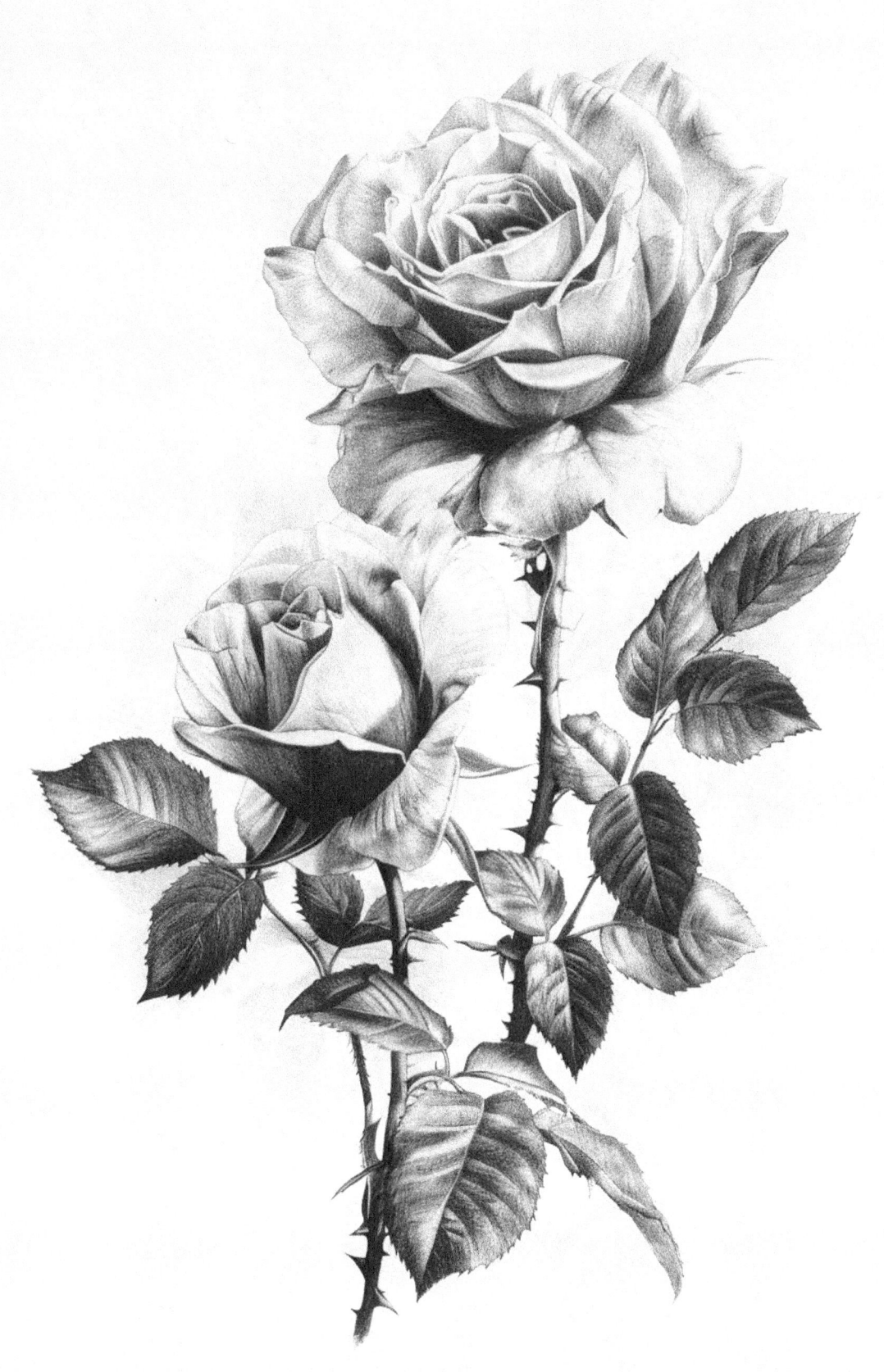

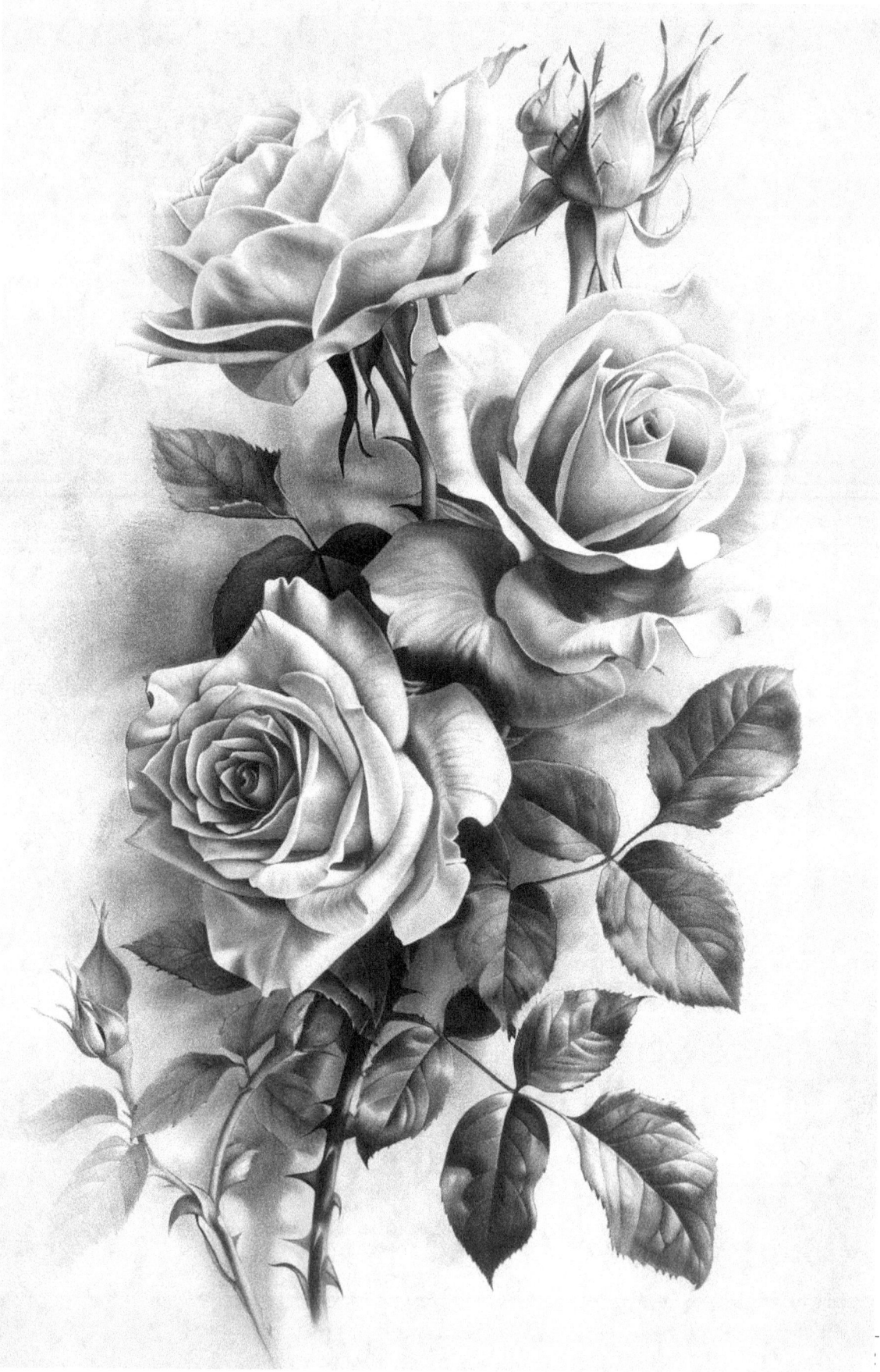

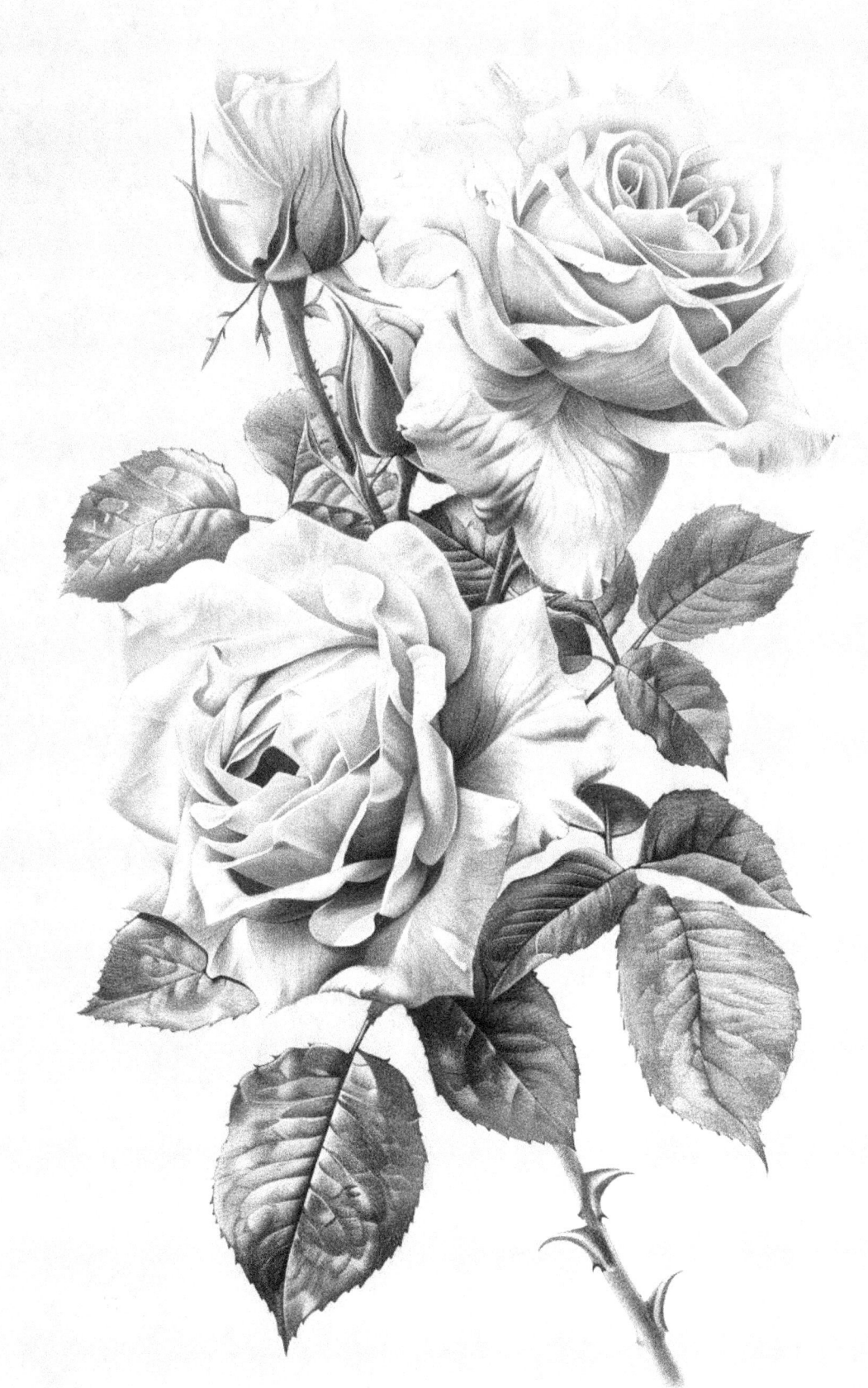

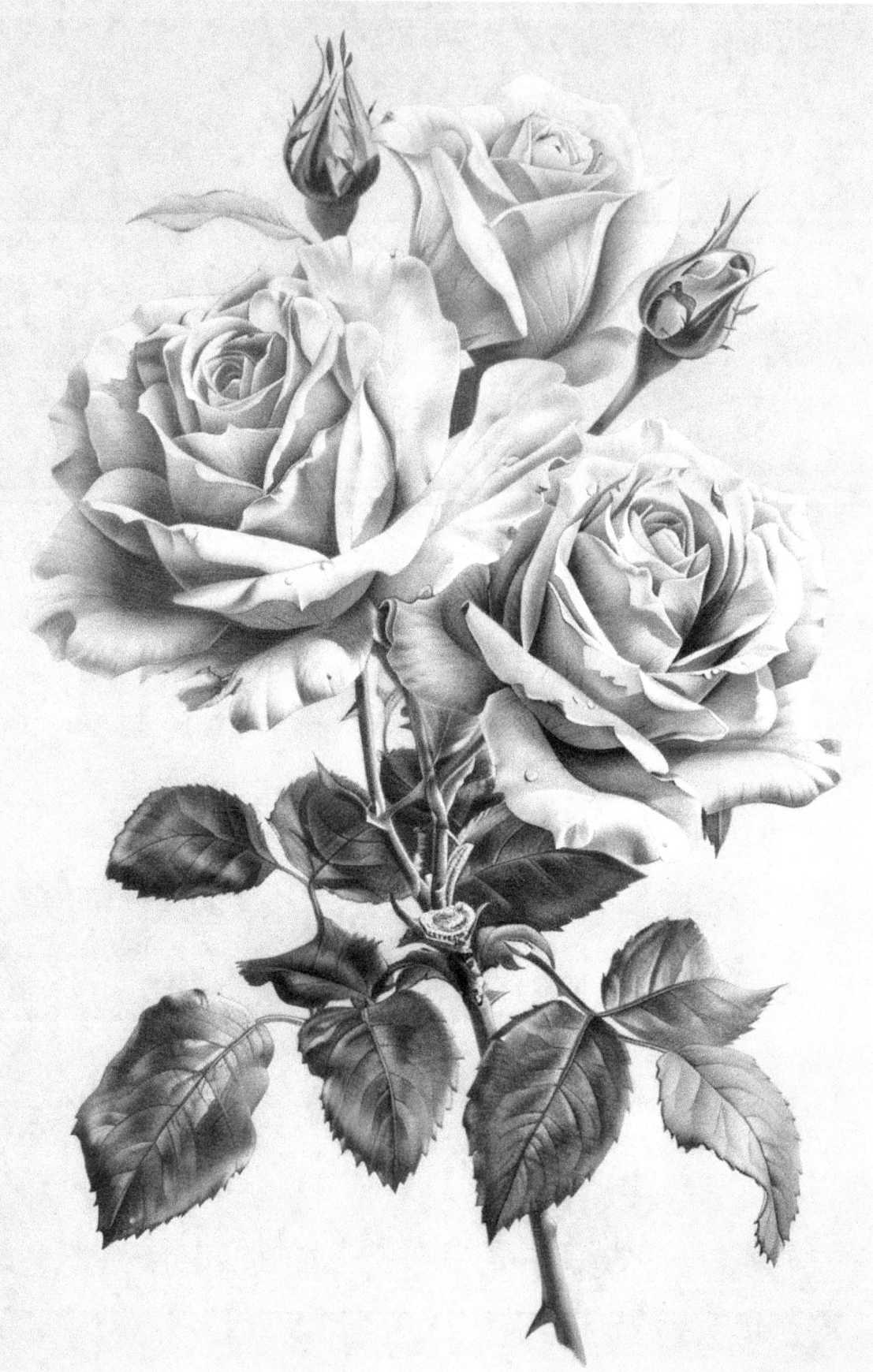

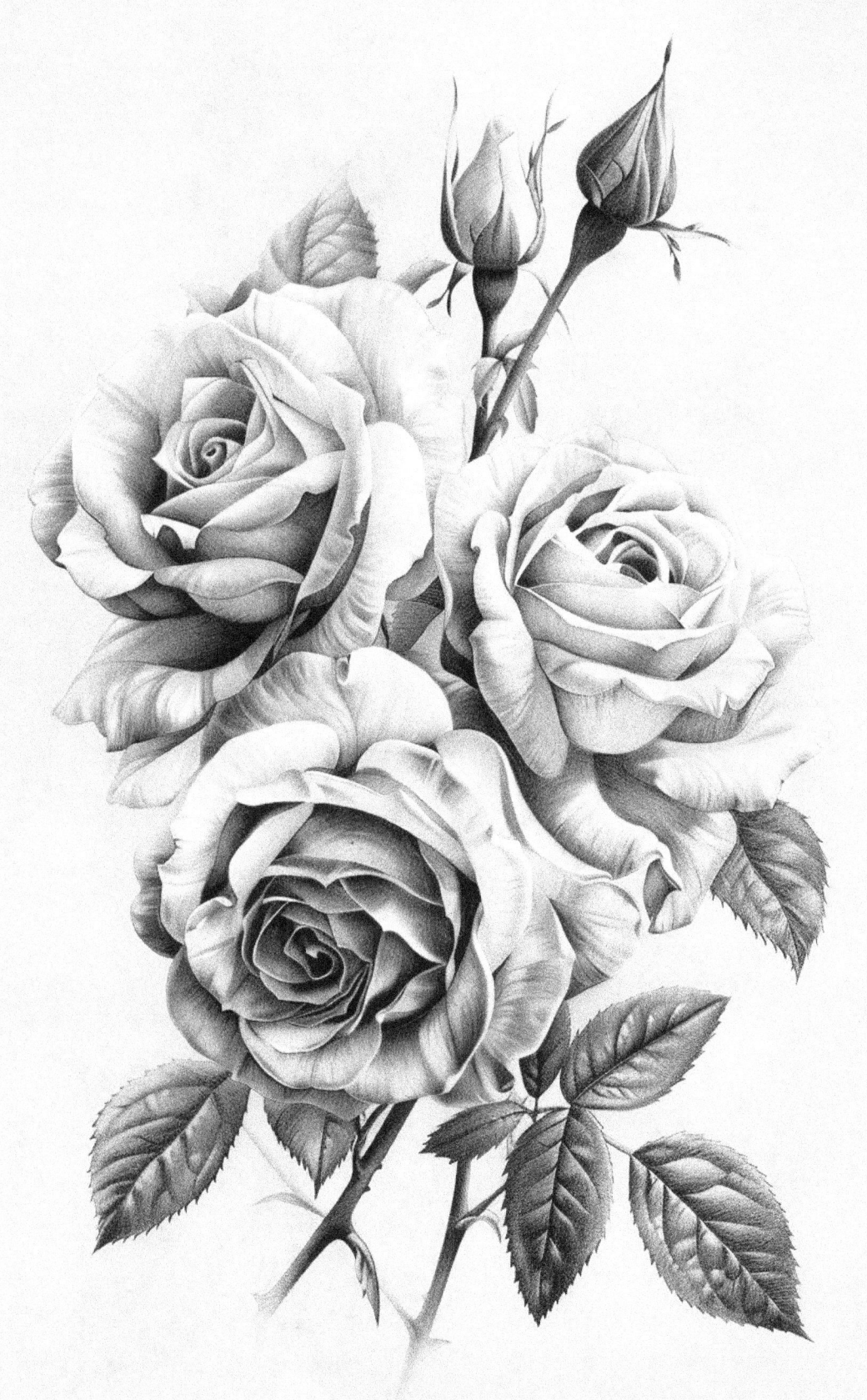

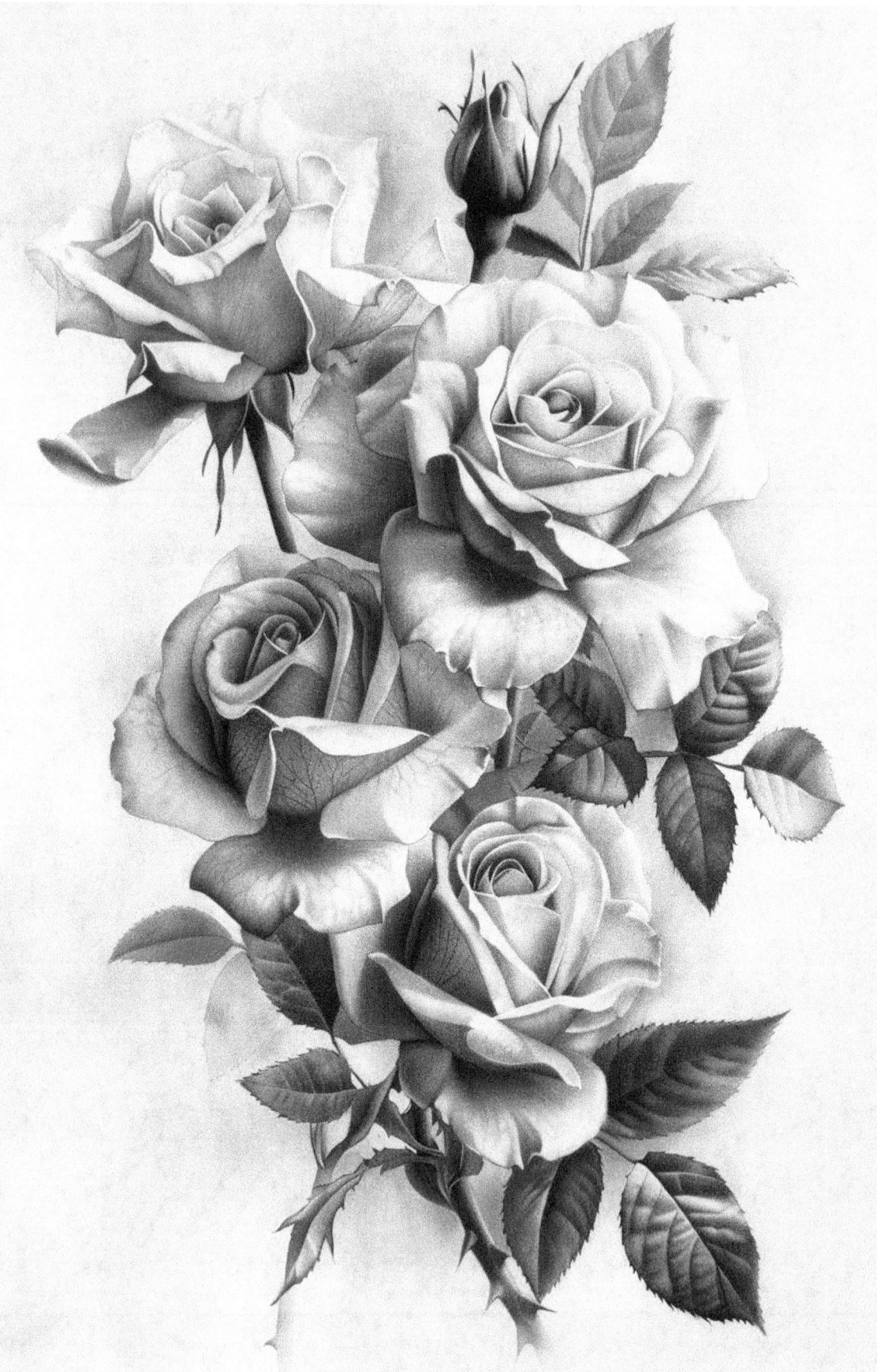

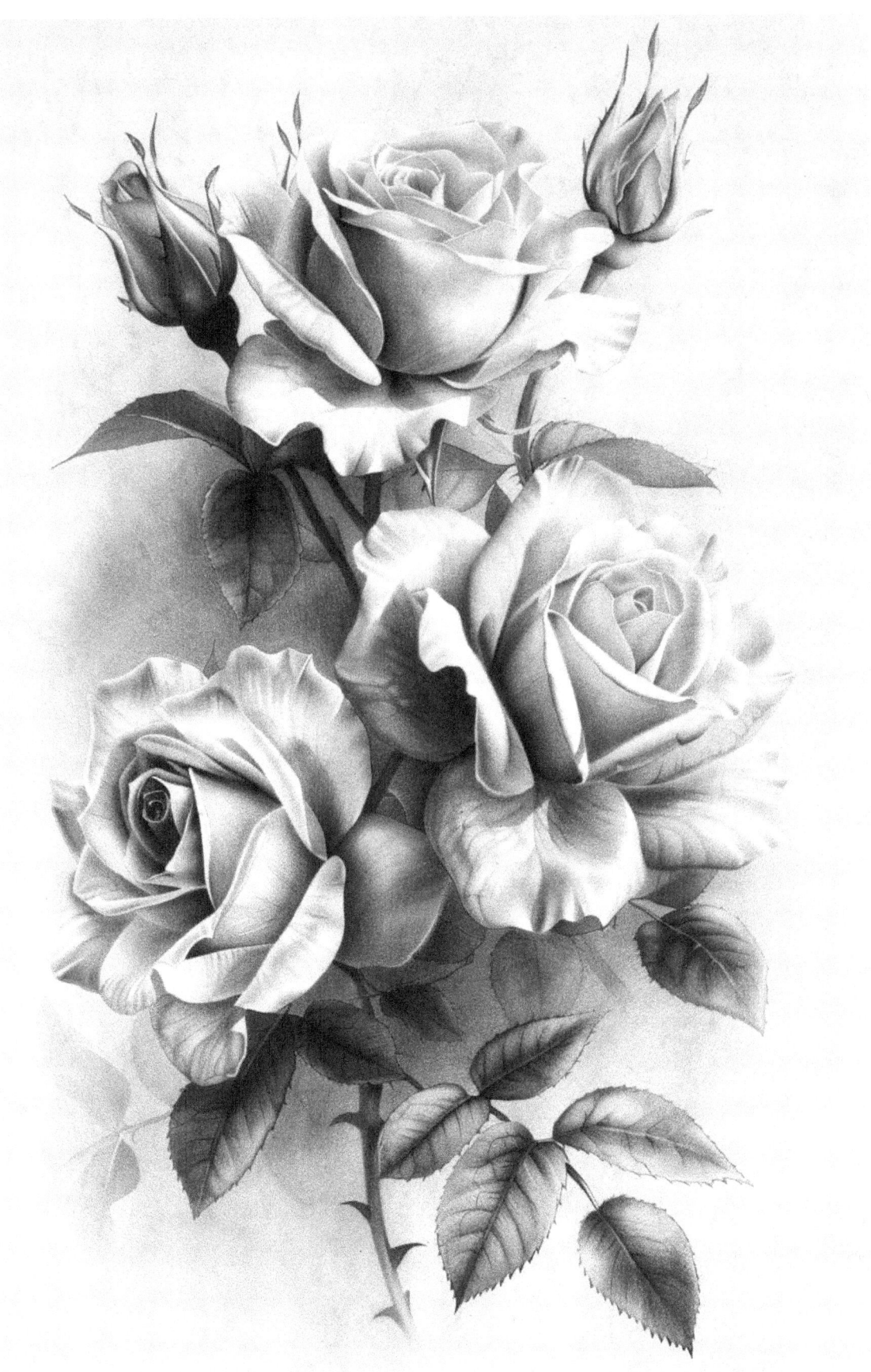

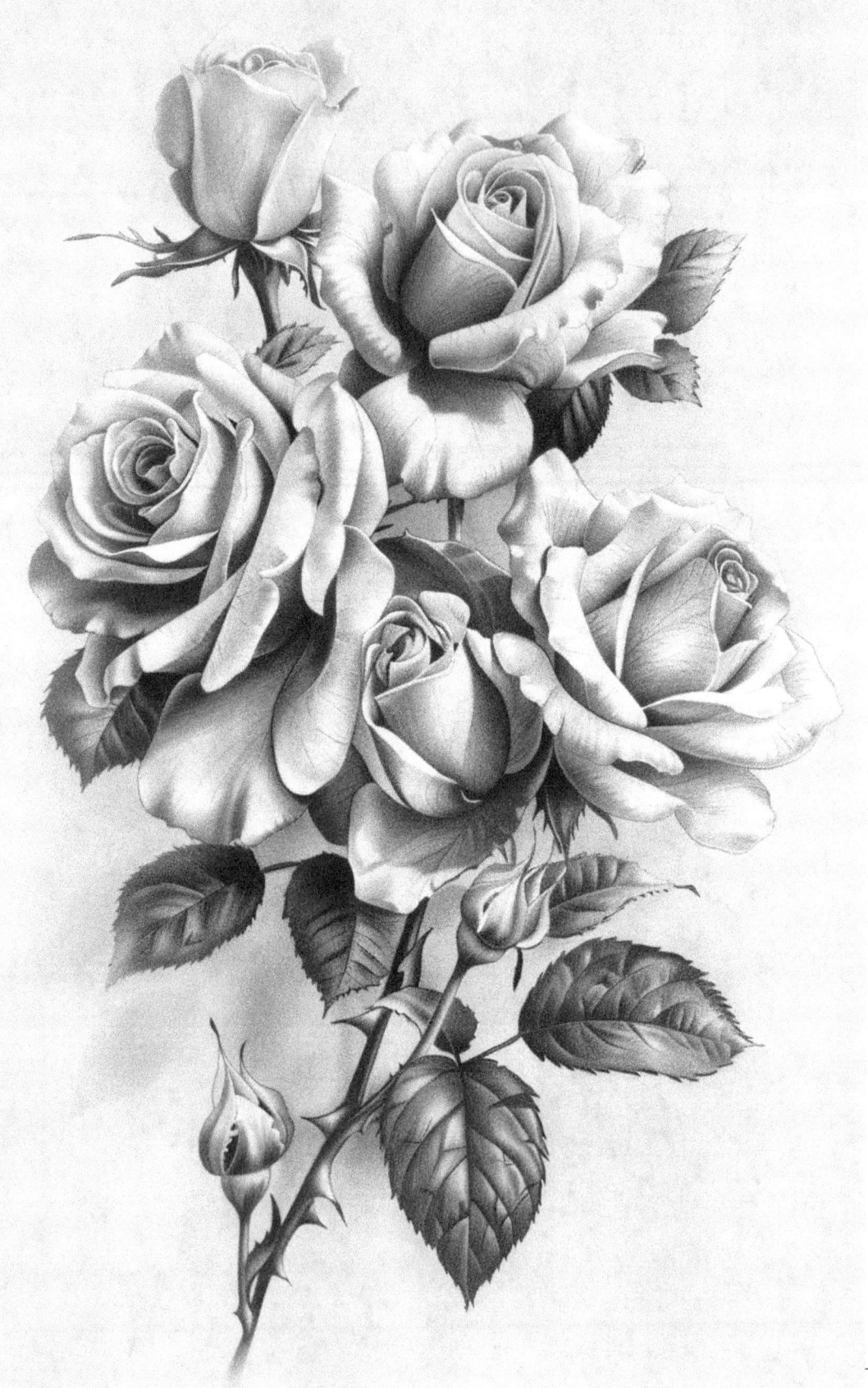

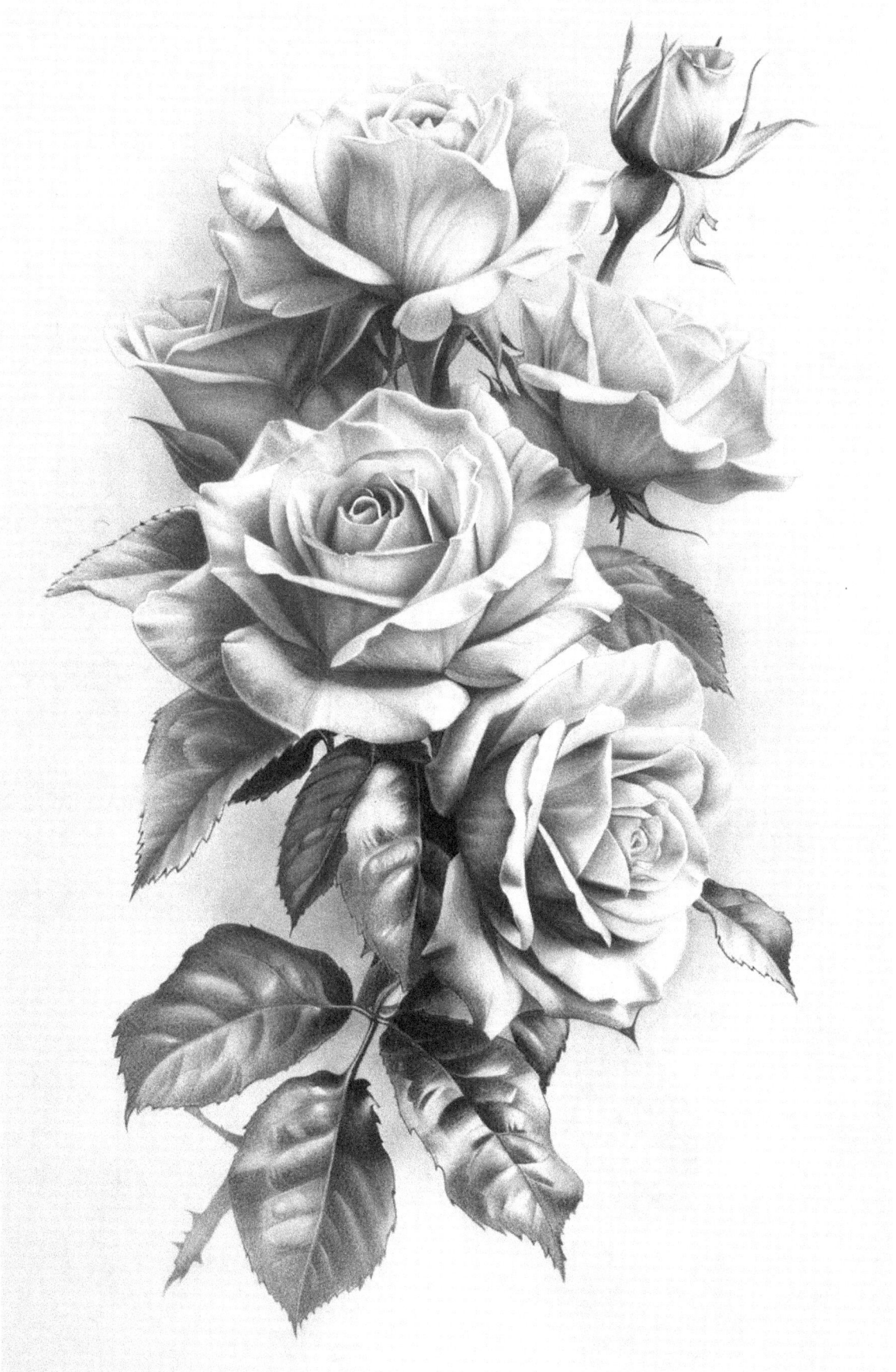

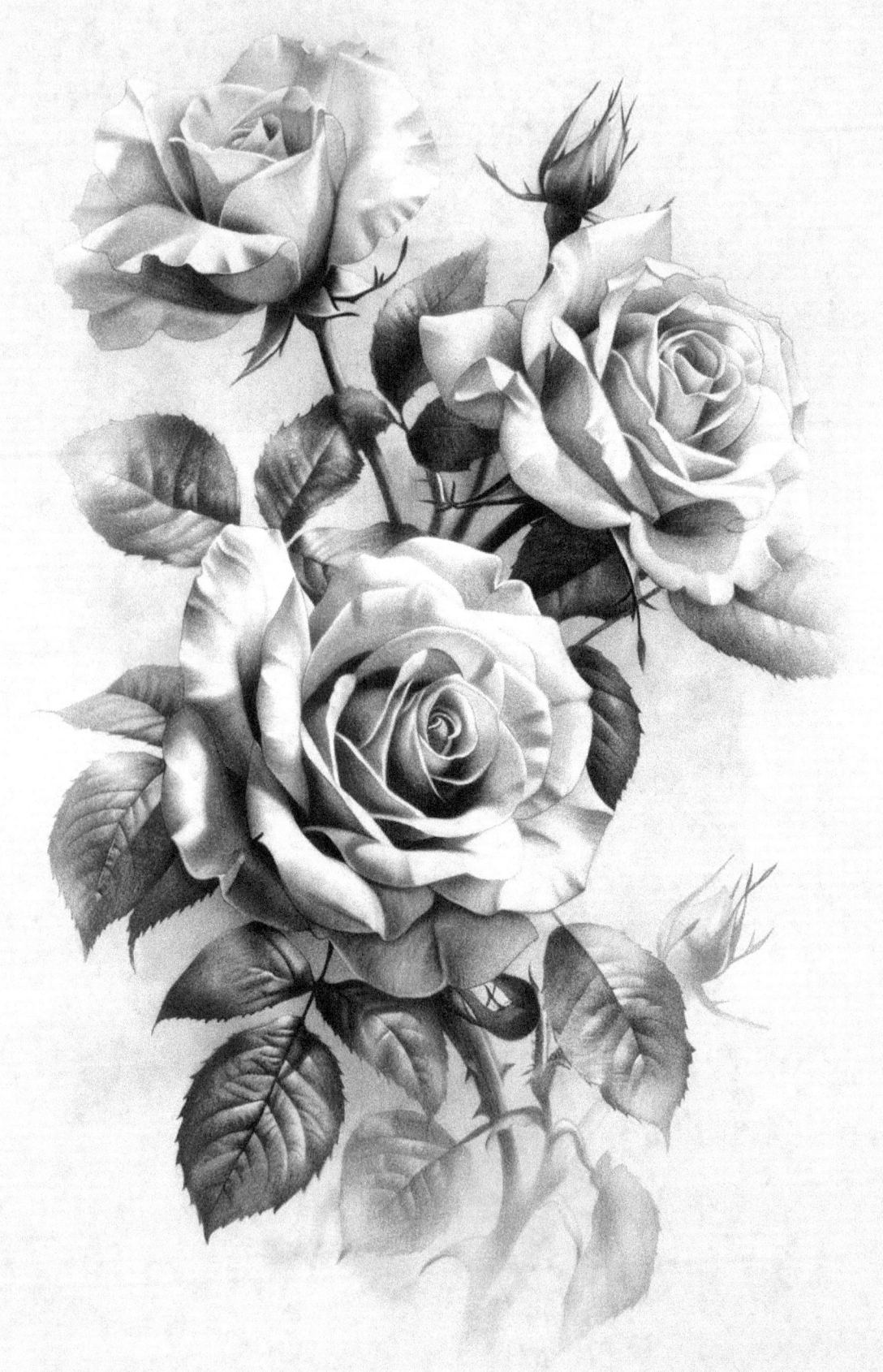

www.ingramcontent.com/pod-product-compliance
Lightning Source LLC
Chambersburg PA
CBHW080958290526
45795CB00009B/2999